D0113722

I Remember Bo

*Memories of Michigan's
Legendary Coach*

George Cantor

TRIUMPH
B O O K S

Copyright © 2007 by George Cantor

No part of this publication may be reproduced, stored in a retrieval system, or transmitted in any form by any means, electronic, mechanical, photocopying, or otherwise, without the prior written permission of the publisher, Triumph Books, 542 South Dearborn Street, Suite 750, Chicago, Illinois 60605.

Triumph Books and colophon are registered trademarks of Random House, Inc.

Library of Congress Cataloging-in-Publication Data

Cantor, George, 1941-
    I remember Bo : memories of Michigan's legendary coach / George Cantor.
        p. cm.
    ISBN-13: 978-1-60078-007-3
    ISBN-10: 1-60078-007-5
    1. Schembechler, Bo. 2. Football coaches—United States—Biography. 3. Michigan Wolverines (Football team)—History. 4. University of Michigan—Football—History. I. Title.

GV939.S33C36 2007
796.332092—dc22
    [B]   2007014876

This book is available in quantity at special discounts for your group or organization. For further information, contact:

Triumph Books
542 South Dearborn Street
Suite 750
Chicago, Illinois 60605
(312) 939-3330
Fax (312) 663-3557

Printed in U.S.A.
ISBN: 978-1-60078-007-3
Design by Patricia Frey
All photos courtesy of Per Kjelden, Bentley Historical Library, University of Michigan; AP/Wide World Photos except where otherwise noted.

Contents

Foreword

Bo Schembechler pulled off one of the greatest charades of all time. He wanted you to think of him as a heartless son of a bitch. He wanted to seem tough and gruff. And it was all a façade.

Behind the mask was one of the warmest, most caring and generous human beings I've ever known. He was a man who truly enjoyed people and carried around an unfailing moral compass.

You can go to the library and pull down all the books on leadership that have ever been written, and Bo was there first. They are all modeled on the things he preached.

What it all comes down to is this: you build a team or an organization on trust. That was the basis of everything he believed. If you could trust everyone around you, you had a team.

Sometimes I think he really started to trust me when I became his regular babysitter. He and Millie would go out and I'd sit with Shemy because my dad's house was right down the street in the same neighborhood.

I was 13 years old and Shemy was about five, and Millie would always tell me if I got tired just to fall asleep on the sofa and not worry about it. They never stayed out late. They were always back by midnight. But he'd walk in and call out, "Jim, you sleepin'?" and I'd always manage to jerk myself awake, even if I'd dozed off. I think he knew that, too, and just wanted to give me some advance warning.

Once when Shemy was over at our house, Bo came by and told him it was time to go home. Shemy refused. Bo repeated it and again Shemy said no. When Bo said it a third time, Shemy threw a block down the stairs and hit him right in the head. I just stood there in fear and waited for the explosion from this ogre. He just chuckled and said, "Kid's got a little spunk."

I was always around his office. He had a huge soft spot for kids, not just for Shemy but all his coaches' kids, too. We had the run of the place and he always made us feel special, always asking us what we were up to.

But when I grew up to be his quarterback, it was strictly business. And when I went ahead and said that we could beat

Jim Harbaugh was a four-year letterman at the University of Michigan and finished his college career in the top five in passing attempts, completions, completion percentage, passing yards, and touchdown passes.

Ohio State if they played the game at midnight in a parking lot, I think I might have upset him a little. He never said so publicly. He backed me up all the way.

Years later, though, Cam Cameron, who was our quarterbacks coach, told me that Bo said to the staff, "We've got a quarterback who's whistling past the graveyard." But he never let me know there were any doubts in his mind.

Of course, if my quarterback this season guarantees a win against California the weekend before the game, I might have some second thoughts about all that.

The things I learned from Bo are ingrained in my DNA. Bo and my dad— coach Jack Harbaugh—molded me. It's not like I sat there and took notes. Just the experience of playing for him put you in the oven and forged you into the iron that he then shaped.

He did that to thousands of people. Even today you can talk to players he kicked off the team and they revere him. They knew in their bones that everything he did was for the good of the team, and even though they suffered for it they understood that. That's quite a testament.

I took so much from Bo when I became a head coach:

1. Winning by the rules is the most important thing. If you cheat, that equates to losing.
2. Work harder than anyone else. If you did it harder and you did it right, you are going to be more successful than your opponent.
3. Make decisions on just two criteria: Will it help us win? Is it good for the team? Everything else is irrelevant and a distraction.

I look back on it and everything he spoke about was *team*. Sometimes you almost felt that you were short-changing yourself for the program and the best interests of the team. But you came to realize that he was right. The team was trust and without that, you have no team.

I realize now how incredibly fortunate I was to have played for him and to have known him as a person, a family man, our neighbor. I just want to carry it forward now and transmit all the things I learned from him to the men who will be playing for me. I think that's the highest honor I can pay to Bo.

—Jim Harbaugh, quarterback, Michigan '86;
Head coach, Stanford University

Preface

Maybe it helps if you understand the times. In the winter of 1968, the country seemed to be coming apart. Dr. Martin Luther King Jr. and Bobby Kennedy had been assassinated. There were riots in Chicago during the Democratic National Convention. The Vietnam protests were deepening in intensity and violence. Ann Arbor was a focus of the anti-war movement, and student demonstrations were an almost daily occurrence. There were calls to armed revolution by half a dozen groups, from the Black Panthers to the Weathermen.

That extended introduction is the best way of explaining the impact Glenn "Bo" Schembechler had when he arrived at Michigan, and the genuine sense of loss that accompanied his death in November 2006.

In an era when we were all being told to do our own thing, whatever that was supposed to mean, and when anyone who advocated a disciplined life was regarded as a fascist, here was this guy who refused to bend. Who was uncompromising in his belief that doing things the tough way was the only right way. Who felt that football was more than a metaphor for life. It was life itself, reduced to a 100-yard battle zone, and there could be no substitutes for preparation, dedication, and, yes, discipline.

If you did not live through those times, you cannot imagine how ludicrous that message sounded on a campus that was halfway to wackyland.

Of course, if Bo hadn't also been a fantastic coach, none of that would have mattered. But he believed in these qualities and managed to translate them into measurable success, and to some degree the lesson took—not only among the players he coached, but also among those who were drawn to the Michigan team. In more recent years, the term *old school* has come into vogue as a way of describing a person or a style that conforms to enduring values. Bo was old school all the way.

In 1968, there also was nothing like the autumn celebration that football in Ann Arbor has become. Most crowds in the Big

Despite the turbulence around his arrival in Ann Arbor, Bo was an unwavering, irresistible force throughout his career.

House were around 60,000. Even the Ohio State game did not sell out. In the 17 seasons between 1951 and 1967, Michigan had a losing record seven times and went to the Rose Bowl only once. The dominant football school was MSU, and Michigan was yesterday's news, wrapped up in a ribbon with Fielding Yost and Fritz Crisler. Bo changed all that.

When I covered his first press conference after he was hired, I never would have guessed I was looking at an icon-to-be. I had been assigned by the *Detroit Free Press* to find out who the next Michigan football coach would be and wrote that Ara Parseghian was the man. As it turned out, he had recommended Bo, as had his former coach, Woody Hayes. Well, at least I was close.

The only knock on Bo was that he never won a national championship. The fact is, however, that the Fates conspired against him.

In 1971, the only time he took an undefeated team to a bowl game, the team was ranked fourth even before losing to Stanford in the Rose Bowl. Nebraska was number one from start to finish in the polls that season and destroyed Alabama in the Orange Bowl, so there was no chance there.

Two years later, after Michigan tied top-ranked Ohio State, 10–10, but was deprived of a chance to play in the Rose Bowl, the Wolverines actually dropped from fourth to sixth in the final poll. Notre Dame won it by defeating Alabama in the Sugar Bowl.

In 1976, they were ranked second with one loss going into the Rose Bowl, but Pittsburgh finished undefeated and was voted number one. Bo's best shot actually might have been his last team, in 1989. He went into the Rose Bowl at number three with one loss. Had Michigan won the game, sentiment might have given him the title. But Michigan lost and Miami, with one loss, was voted in.

The Fates conspired.

I interviewed him a few times during his years at Michigan. He always associated me with being a baseball writer and each time I entered his office he would growl, "Now why would George Cantor want to write anything about football?" Then he'd talk football for as long as I wanted to stay.

I wrote some tough things about him during the time when legendary announcer Ernie Harwell was fired while Bo was president of the Detroit Tigers. That annoyed him, I'm sure. But once it was over, it was over, and I think that was a constant in his life.

He was a man for all seasons, but autumn is when he truly came alive. Although the man is gone, the stories will live on as long as they play "The Victors" and Michigan teams run out of the tunnel into the sunlight at the Big House and the cheers of 110,000 of the Maize and Blue faithful. I am not a big fan of blogs, but reading over hundreds of them that followed the announcement of his death brought tears to my eyes. No matter which side you were on in the big games, you realized that a giant had left us.

This book has pulled together some of the best of the stories, from those who knew him best, told in their own words. His influence on the Michigan program, through his own coaching tenure and those of his protégés, Gary Moeller and Lloyd Carr, is in its 39th year. That is longer than the dynasties of either Yost or Crisler were perpetuated. Michigan players in team meetings are still told to put both feet on the floor and look straight ahead when the coach is talking, just as Bo demanded.

I wish I could say I knew him better. When I was writing a magazine piece on a Michigan fantasy football camp in the summer of 2006, a photographer took a picture of the two of us together. Bo looked at me in amusement and I could almost hear him say to himself, "What's that baseball guy doing here?"

I'm not especially sentimental about these things, but I'm going to save that picture. I guess I just told you why.

Acknowledgments

It was not an easy task to track down and interview in such a short time span so many of the players and coaches associated with the life and career of Bo Schembechler. I'd like to thank the Michigan Letterwinners M Club, especially Pam Stevens and Dave Rentschler, for their invaluable assistance in doing this.

Recognition must also go to my sportswriting class at Oakland University. The contributions of these young journalists is irreplaceable and they should be mentioned by name. They are Mike Caravaggio, Kevin Coil, Samantha Franz, Elizabeth Glynn, Matt Goricki, Paul Gully, Aaron Hanke, Justin Howland, Vicky LeFebvre, Patrick Leonhard, Ryan Moskwa, Brittany Ochtinsky, Dave Phillips, Adam Roberts, Jake Sharfman, Matt Wright, and Jake Zammit. On this assignment, they all deserved an "A."

The staff at the *Detroit News* library, headed by Pat Zacharias, was also enormously helpful with the research involved.

CHAPTER 1

Beginnings at Barberton

The town is named for the president of a match company. That was one of the few flashes of light Barberton, Ohio, ever saw. It was and remains a hardworking, tough, blue-collar town on the southwestern fringe of Akron. About a quarter of its 25,000 residents are of German descent, like Glenn Schembechler. Tough-minded people who know value when they see it, and are pretty big on values, too.

Barberton is also situated near the historic heart of Ohio football country. It is a few miles up the road from the birthplace of the National Football League in Canton. The town where legendary coach Paul Brown established his storied high school program at Massillon is just down the Tuscarawas Valley. Football is part of the air you breathe in these places.

"I came from Barberton, too, and I knew what it was like to grow up there. When Bo arrived at Michigan in my sophomore year he called me into his office. I just sat there for five minutes in total silence while he was writing in a notebook. Occasionally he'd peer up at me, but he never said a word and I was getting more and more nervous. We'd been going through some tough workouts and I thought he'd heard about the discontent that was being voiced and was holding me responsible.

Despite his affinity for his hometown of Barberton, Ohio, and fellow natives like Billy Taylor, Bo was admittedly harder on them than other players.

"Finally, he looked up at me and said, 'Taylor, you know I'm going to have to be harder on you than anyone else. I can't have people think I'm playing favorites just because we're both from Barberton.' Believe me, he was as good as his word."

Billy Taylor
running back, 1971

"After my graduation we'd go on road trips together sometimes. This one time somehow we ended up back in Barberton. He was just a different person while we were there.

"His eyes lit up and he showed me his old snow hill and the field where he played football, the spot where he got dragged through a tomato patch trying to make a tackle but refused to let go.

"'When I was in middle school,' he said, 'there weren't enough players to field a team. So if I wanted to scrimmage I had to go over to the high school team. They knocked the snot out of me. But it toughened me up. I never was intimidated by anything after that.

"'Then I played tackle in college at Miami and we went to the Salad Bowl in 1950 against Arizona State. I was lined up against a guy who'd been named to some All-America teams and must have outweighed me by almost 50 pounds. I handled him. That was the Barberton coming out.'

"He told me how his little sister gave him his nickname when she tried to say 'brother' and it came out 'Bobo.' I'd never seen him before the way he was on that day in Barberton. It was like he was letting the little kid in him come out again. He couldn't do that when he was a coach. I don't know that he allowed many people to see that side of him. That was a pretty great day."

Jamie Morris
running back, 1987

"He liked to tell the story about when his dad was applying for the job of fire chief in Barberton. There was a written exam, and Bo's father was told by his buddies at the Elks

Jamie Morris saw a softer side of Bo during a visit to their hometown of Barberton.

Club that his competitor had somehow obtained a copy of the test beforehand. His dad was then given the opportunity to get his hands on the exam, too.

"Bo said that he absolutely refused, and as a result he never got the job. He refused to work for the guy who cheated, too, and quit the department rather than do that. You don't have to have an advanced degree to see the effect that had on him as a coach and as a man. If you didn't do things the right way, whatever you may achieve is going to be empty. That's what he sincerely believed and it's the whole idea in a nutshell of what he instilled in the young men who played for him.

"And it wasn't just talk. Once I got him to appear at a charity outing at Lochmoor Country Club, in Grosse Pointe. He refused to take any honorarium. I felt bad about that, so in the prize drawings after dinner we rigged it so that he would win a shotgun. Somehow he found out that his name was the only one that had been written on the slips of paper that were drawn. He returned the gun immediately and said there was no way he could take it."

Dave Rentschler
end, 1956, and former
M Club president, 1978–79

"When we went out on recruiting trips, the timing was always tight. It seemed we were forever trying to catch up to the schedule, and there were plenty of days we couldn't even stop to eat.

"Bo would take it for a while, but as the afternoon wore on he'd just keep getting grouchier and grouchier. I'd be driving and finally he'd grab my arm and say, 'Hanlon, if you drive past one more Wendy's, I'll fire you.'

"On one of these trips, he started reaching this point and he suddenly asked me how far we were from Barberton. I said we were going to pass right by it on the Ohio turnpike. 'Well, what if we don't get on the turnpike,' he says.

"'Bo, what do you want me to do?' I asked. 'Jerry,' he said. 'You know damn well what I want you to do.' He had a special place in his heart for this place in Barberton called the Belgrade Gardens. It served the most deliciously unhealthy deep-fried chicken with the skin still on, with french fries and coleslaw.

"For a man with his heart problems there were probably few meals that could have been worse. But whenever we got anywhere near Barberton, he insisted that we go there. The funny thing was he made it sound every time like it was some spur of the moment kind of thing and I know he'd been thinking about it for days.

"But he was a great actor and a lot of the things he did in practice that seemed to be spontaneous had been absolutely calculated to get a specific effect at that particular time. Every time he'd do it, I'd say to myself, 'Belgrade Gardens.'"

Jerry Hanlon
assistant coach, 1969–91

CHAPTER
2

The Arrival

Bo took over a good Michigan team that went 8–2 during the 1968 season. After an opening loss to California, it reeled off eight wins in a row before playing undefeated Ohio State in Columbus for the Big Ten Championship. The result was a 50–14 throttling. Even though Bump Elliot had taken Michigan to its only Rose Bowl in 18 years in 1964, he was gone, bumped up to assistant athletics director. No Michigan coach could survive that score.

So the cupboard wasn't exactly bare when Bo walked in, and he acknowledged that readily. All-Americans such as Dan Dierdorf, Reggie McKenzie, and Billy Taylor were already in place. In fact, when Bo became president of the declining Detroit Tigers in 1990 one of the things he said was, "Bump, where are you?"

Still, there was no question the Michigan program was down. In most seasons since 1950 the team had finished in the middle of the pack in the Big Ten. Only twice was it ranked in the top 10 nationally at season's end. A sellout was rare at the Big House, even for the Buckeyes. It was a program that reeked of lassitude.

Fritz Crisler had come to Michigan in 1938 and the next two coaches, Bennie Oosterbaan and Elliot, were his lineal descendants in football philosophy. At last, 30 years later, athletics director Don Canham decided it was finally time to go outside the family. He solicited opinions from many of the top coaches in the country, and his search finally led him to Miami University in Oxford, Ohio.

He was the darkest of dark horse candidates. When he was registered at an Ann Arbor hotel as "Glenn Schems" the night before he was to be introduced as head coach no one had an inkling who he was. The problem was neither did Bo. When he went to check in at the hotel he forgot the name he was supposed to give.

No one was quite sure how to pronounce his name at the press conference, either. "You can call me anything you want," he said. "How does Field Marshal sound?"

"They didn't have to sell me on anything," he said. "I knew why I was here. As for the money, it was $1,000 a year more than I was making at Miami. I would have come for less."

When Bo (pictured at left with athletic director Don Canham and football legend Bump Elliott) was hired in 1969, the media struggled with pronouncing his name at the press conference.

Over the previous six seasons as head coach at Miami he had gone 40–17–3 and won two Mid-American Conference titles. But this staunch Ohioan was about to become the ultimate Michigan Man. There was one final problem, though. When he and his staff of assistants arrived in Ann Arbor in a caravan of cars in January, no one knew how to find the athletic department offices. The new coach had to stop, find a pay phone, and call for directions before he could officially go on the job.

When they finally got there and started to inspect the facilities, one of his assistants began to grouse at how cramped and dark the coaches' dressing area was. "How can you say that?" Bo demanded. "Don't you realize that hook on the wall is the same one that Fielding Yost hung his clothes on?"

"I'd been on the Michigan staff for 17 or 18 years and I knew what the problems were with the football program. I knew I was going to hire a coach. I thought I was going to hire Joe Paterno because, to tell you the truth, he was a friend of mine when I was a track coach.

"Paterno was the only guy I offered the job to. Schembechler always claimed I offered it to everybody in the country before I got to him, but that's not true. I may have talked to everybody in the country but the only guy I offered it to was Paterno.

"Joe was just another great young coach in those days, and he'd only been head coach at Penn State for three years. But he didn't want to make a decision until after his bowl game and I told him I couldn't wait that long. Meanwhile, in the conversations I was having with people, Bo's name kept coming up.

"Bo had the background, head coaching experience, knowledge of the Big Ten. He was a winner. His personality just struck me right away. I hired him 15 minutes after we began to talk. That was the turning point in my career as an athletics director. That's because he started winning right away. We didn't have to wait four, five years."

Don Canham
late Michigan athletics director

"The first meeting with Bo was intolerable. I was a senior when he arrived and he met with our class first of all. He looked at my 5'10" frame and he said, 'You started here last year? I can't believe it.' I couldn't believe it, either. How many times did I have to prove myself? I'd had to do it with every coach I ever played for before, and now here comes another one.

"So I said to him, 'Yeah, I started and I can play. Watch the films.' He just stared back at me and said, 'I will watch the films.' I figured I had just screwed myself, mouthing off on my first meeting with the coach. But that's the kind of kid I was.

"Later on, one of the assistant coaches told me that was just the response he'd been looking for from this team. He wanted players who would spit back at him. He wanted players who weren't going to be intimidated and back down. The testing had begun even before he had us on the practice field for the first time.

"At the next meeting, he reads off my name and says, 'You're Italian, right? Woody Hayes told me never to start Italians because they're selfish people. Is that true?'

"If a coach said anything like that today he'd have a dozen groups calling for him to be fired the next day. I guess it does sound offensive, but I always thought it was funny. It was all just part of the weeding-out process."

Rich Caldarazzo
offensive lineman, 1969

"Bo really tried hard to recruit me at Miami and it was tough to tell him that I had chosen Michigan. Then he arrived in Ann Arbor about the same way that General Patton arrived in Europe. He was not exactly an inconspicuous person.

"When he walked into that first meeting, I went up to him with my hand out. You know, let's shake and renew old acquaintances.

"He just looked at my hand, grabbed my stomach instead, and said, 'You're fat, you're mine, and I never forget a snub.'"

Dan Dierdorf
offensive lineman, 1970

"Thom Darden and I made our campus visit to Miami together. We were looking for it to be a fun weekend and we'd gone out with some members of the team late on a Friday night. At 6:00 the next morning there was a banging on our door. I thought it was a joke and kind of went stumbling over to answer it and give it back to whomever it was I saw there.

"It was Bo and he was yelling at us to get our asses out of bed. He took us out on the football field and had us doing wind sprints. That was followed by weightlifting and then a full-court basketball drill.

Dan Dierdorf resisted Bo's recruiting efforts when Bo was still at Miami of Ohio, but was unceremoniously reunited with the coach when Bo accepted the top job at Michigan.

"Darden and I both thought the man was crazy and crossed Miami right off our lists. I had some feelers from Ohio State and even Cornell, but Michigan looked like the best fit for me. That's where Darden wound up, too. I loved Bump Elliot and my first semester in Ann Arbor was great.

"Then I opened the newspaper in December 1968 and my heart sank. 'Schembechler named Michigan coach.' I thought someone was playing a cruel joke on me."

Billy Taylor
running back, 1971

"I grew up in Ohio and Bo hadn't even tried to recruit me when he was at Miami. So I didn't know what was going to happen when he took over at Michigan. Well, maybe I did know because I heard from friends that it was not going to be fun when he got there.

"I'd been playing fullback on the freshman team for Bump, but Bo watched the film and decided that I had the ability to play strong side safety, or the Wolfman. Of course, he never told me that. He just kept harping on my size. I only weighed 185 pounds and he kept calling me 'Lollipop.' Even when I kept busting up his power sweeps in practice it was always 'Lollipop.'

"But you lived to see a smile on his face. He usually didn't say much if everything was going right. But he'd smile. You'd look for that smile and when it was there everything was rosy. When I was named a captain in my senior year it was really a culmination of everything he had been psyching me up to. He dropped the Lollipop stuff long before that."

Frank Gusich
defensive back, 1971

"We must have started with about 150 guys when he came here. After spring practice we were down to 75 or 80. A lot of players resented Bo because he was so damn demanding. But it was a strong group who stayed."

Jim Betts
quarterback, 1970

"When you'd go to his office first thing in the morning and he'd already be watching films, or you'd see him doing the same thing on Saturday night when the rest of us were off...well, you'd start to say to yourself, 'If he can do it maybe the rest of us better stop complaining and make up our minds that we can do it, too.'"

Jim Mandich
tight end and captain, 1969

"I was a walk-on and I really came to Michigan for its industrial engineering program. Football was kind of an afterthought for me, something I'd look into. Then Bo came there in my sophomore year and he scared the hell out of us.

"He let us know that this team was not playing up to its potential and by God he was going to get that potential out of us. That was his responsibility. Then he started laying out the new rules and let us know what our responsibilities would be.

"Up until then we thought our responsibilities were to show up for practice on time and go to class. Bo wasn't buying any of that. From now on, just for starters, freshmen and sophomores had to live in university housing and married players had to live in married student housing. We thought he was kidding. But he was dead serious.

"That's when a lot of the walk-ons decided they didn't want to play football at Michigan anymore."

Fritz Seyferth
running back, 1971

"He beat the crap out of us those first few months of 1969. The walk-ons were dropping like flies. We had to run a mile in under six minutes, jump the stadium stairs on one leg, then jump upstairs on one leg with a teammate on your back.

Tight end and team captain Jim Mandich felt Bo set a great example for his teams by striving for constant improvement.

"We hated it and we hated him. But you know what—that was exactly what we were looking for."

Rich Caldarazzo
offensive lineman, 1969

"These were all someone else's players. Bo didn't recruit them. He had to find out in a hurry who he could count on and who he could trust. He set out to make sure the others left. That's why he put up that famous sign: 'Those Who Stay Will Be Champions.' Everyone who ever played for Bo always remembers that sign."

Dave Rentschler
former M Club president, 1978–79

"One of the players who decided to leave put up an addition under that sign with magic marker. It read: 'And those who don't will be doctors, lawyers, and business giants.' Years later, Bo was speaking to a group of businessmen and asked: 'Being business people what do you expect that guy is doing today? He's probably a lawyer.'"

Jerry Hanlon
assistant coach, 1969–91

"Bo came into the first staff meeting and laid out a very simple goal. He said, 'We are here at Michigan to beat one and only one team—Woody Hayes and Ohio State.'

"In the fifth game of the season he lost to Michigan State, 23–12. Well, of course, the newspapers all over the state were in an uproar about how old Duffy Daugherty had shown up the new guy in Ann Arbor. There were the old jokes about his name sounding like someone who owns a butcher shop, not a football coach.

"Growing up in Ohio, I don't think Bo realized that in Michigan losing to State was also a very big deal. At the next staff meeting he said, 'We are now here to beat two teams.'

"He beat State the next eight times in a row and never lost to Duffy again."

Jim Young
assistant coach, 1969–72

CHAPTER 3

Michigan 24, Ohio State 12

Michigan hadn't sold out the Big House for the Ohio State game since 1957, while the game was never played before less than capacity in Columbus. Since that season, Michigan had gone 3–9 against the Buckeyes. Twice in that span, Woody Hayes had run up 50 points on the Wolverines.

Two years before Bo's first game against Woody, just 64,000 people had been in Ann Arbor to watch OSU win 24–14.

So athletics director Don Canham decided he could fill some empty seats by offering 23,000 tickets to Ohio State to sell for the 1969 game. Hundreds of thousands of Michigan fans might claim to have been there on that November afternoon. But almost one-quarter of the Big House was wearing scarlet and gray that day.

The next week, Bo went into Canham's office and said: "Never do that to me again." And he never did. He never had to.

> "Bo posted that score of the 1968 game on every one of our lockers. Ohio State 50, Michigan 14. I played in that '68 game and it isn't likely that any of us who did would ever forget what had happened. He also stenciled the score on the sleeves of the scout team and taped up a picture of every Ohio State player who would be lined up opposite each of us.

Ohio State fans filled nearly a quarter of the seats in the Big House for the 1969 game, but the Wolverines still prevailed 24–12.

"Bo just wanted it to be in front of us all the time. It was beautiful what he did. His motivational thought process didn't lack anything for that game.

"Ohio State had just crushed everyone they played. No one came within four touchdowns of them all year. The week before us they beat a real good Purdue team 42–14. The Purdue coach, Jack Mollenkopf, said the only other team with a defense that good was the Minnesota Vikings.

"All Bo had to say before the game itself were two words: 'It's time.'"

Barry Pierson
defensive back, 1969

"We still weren't filling the stadium in the first part of that season. Not even close. They had to hold promotions like Band Day just to get some bodies in there.

"We played a pretty good schedule, too. Washington and Missouri in nonconference games, and Missouri just clobbered us, 40–17. It was one of the worst losses Bo ever had at Michigan. Then two weeks later we got smoked by Michigan State and we were 3–2. But Bo never let us lose our focus. It was Ohio State all the time.

"You look back on that year and you think that enthusiasm was building as we started going on a run. But I looked it up once and the last home game before Ohio State was against Wisconsin. It was Homecoming, too. And there were just 60,000 people there.

"We seniors had never beaten Ohio State, and we were a desperate bunch when we ran on that field. The week before we'd beaten Iowa something like 51–6, and everyone in the locker room was chanting 'Beat the Bucks. Beat the Bucks' after the game. One of the coaches went up to Bo and told him he was worried that we were getting too high too soon. 'Naw,' he said, 'let 'em get higher.'

"I don't know why Woody went for the two-point conversion at the end of the 1968 game. If he was trying to rub it in—make the defeat seem worse—then I don't have any respect for that. It certainly wasn't necessary. We weren't going to come roaring back to beat him. But I'll tell you, we never forgot it. If we had scored another touchdown in 1969 we were going for two points, no matter what the coaches would have wanted."

Jim Mandich
tight end, 1969

"After we went for a two-point conversion at the end of the 1968 game, the story was that someone asked Woody why he did it and he said: 'Because I couldn't go for three.' I just don't believe that ever happened. In fact, it

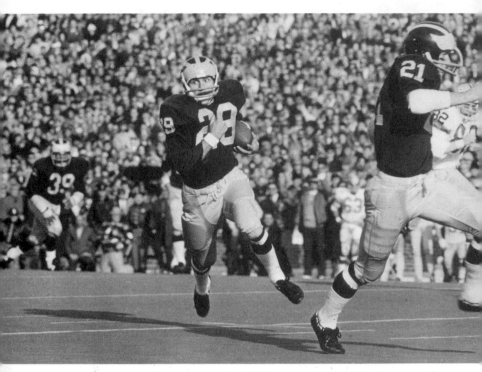

Barry Pierson, shown here in the 1969 game against Ohio State, recalls that Bo wouldn't let his team forget the 1968 loss to the Buckeyes.

wouldn't surprise me if I found out that Bo had made it up to get his team even more riled at us.

"The truth is that two-point conversion was on me. We had scored with our second stringers on the field and they were all jumping up and down, all excited about scoring on Michigan. I looked at the clock and saw that we didn't have enough time to get the kicking team on the field. I didn't want to call a timeout because I thought that would really be rubbing it in.

"So I got us lined up real fast and went for the two and we didn't make it. There's another misperception. People think we did make the two points and that's how we got to 50. But we already had the 50 before we ever tried the conversion.

"Woody never would have done that. It wasn't in the man's character."

Jim Otis
Ohio State fullback, 1969

"We went out there for the pregame warm-ups and Woody had his team on our side of the field. It was no mistake. He'd played in Ann Arbor enough times to know which side was which.

"Bo ran right up to him and told him to get his team over to their own damn side. And we knew right then that we were never going to be intimidated by any team ever again."

Billy Taylor
running back, 1971

"Ohio State came into that game with a 22-game winning streak. They were being called a superteam. Defending national champions. Beat O.J. Simpson and that Southern California bunch in the Rose Bowl. We were 17-point underdogs and a lot of people thought that was being too generous toward us.

"But, honest to God, Bo was mad that we weren't the favorites. He went over their starting lineup man for man and showed us how we were better. He was absolutely confident that he would win, and that sense of confidence went all through our team. No one let down for a single play in that game. I've looked over that film with a fine-tooth comb and every guy played a tremendous game. And I mean end to end for 60 minutes. It didn't matter who we were playing, we would have won.

"You see, Bo knew what Woody knew. He hadn't changed things that much in the years since Bo had been an assistant there. He knew that when Woody called a certain defensive shift it would open our tight end Jim Mandich for a quick pass. Our quarterback, Don Moorhead, hit him every time. He also knew that the key to beating Ohio State was to force Rex Kern to pass, and that was our game plan."

Barry Pierson
defensive back, 1969

"If Woody had a downfall it was that in close games he got too predictable. But in this case he tried to out-think himself. He knew Bo would stack the tackles against the run. So we tried to pass and that wasn't our game. It backfired."

Jim Stillwagon
Ohio State linebacker, 1970

"I swear it was like Bo was in our huddle. He knew everything we were going to do. When did I get over it? I never did."

Rex Kern
Ohio State quarterback, 1970

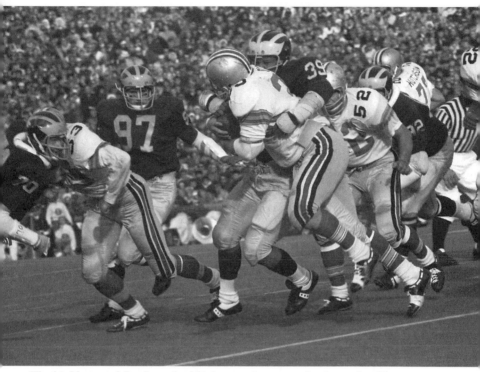

The highly touted Buckeyes had little running room thanks to the efforts of Henry Hill (39) and an inspired Wolverines defense.

"We started moving right through them on our first series of downs just the way Bo said we would. I looked around and we were all thinking, 'Damn, we can beat these guys.'

"Then Bo called 'Dark 26,' which was the same off-tackle blast that Woody had been running for years, and I scored the first touchdown with it. We were sending a message. I said after the game that it was the greatest victory in the history of the world, and I still believe that today."

Garvie Craw
fullback, 1969

"We controlled the game in the second half. It was 24–12 at the break and in the locker room the defense was screaming 'No more points. No more points.' The Ohio State guys were red in the face all through the second half, like they'd just been hit a blow to the stomach.

"I thought back to all those stupid conditioning drills and realized this is what it all was for. They couldn't keep up with us."

Rich Caldarazzo
offensive lineman, 1969

"I was one of those who questioned Bo's methods when he came in. What did I know? I was a 19-year-old kid. We won that game because he made us afraid to lose.

"We had beaten the best Woody had, and some were calling it the best team in the history of college football. That one game vaulted the Michigan program into something exceptional, and it hasn't stopped to this day. We walked off the field after that game and not one of us ever thought of ourselves in the same way again. That's what Bo did."

Dan Dierdorf
offensive lineman, 1970

"I have never looked at that film. I have never discussed it with any of my teammates. It would hurt too much. It was a day when we did everything wrong."

Jim Otis
Ohio State fullback, 1969

"Bo was directly responsible for my getting a degree. I was attending Ohio State in 1969 and planned to drop out of school to take a job on a newspaper. But I was so upset over that game I knew I had to be in Ohio Stadium for payback in 1970.

"The only problem was that there were no tickets available unless you were a student and I had to be enrolled as a student to get one of those. So I stayed in school and got my diploma just so I could see Woody get his revenge. I should have thanked Bo for that but I never did."

Alan Whitt
journalist

"Many years later, Bo went down to Columbus for a private banquet. It was just Woody and some of his former players. Woody got up to speak and began on how great that '69 team was. He stopped, looked over at Bo, and said, 'Damn you, Bo, you'll never win a bigger game than that one.'

"The thing Bo felt the best about was right after the game he got a call from Fritz Crisler, who was in the hospital and couldn't be there. He just wanted to tell Bo how proud he was to be a Michigan man on that day."

Jerry Hanlon
assistant coach, 1969–91

Recruiting

"We do not recruit players. Players recruit Michigan."

Fritz Crisler
Michigan head coach, 1938–47

"The first player I can ever remember being recruited at Michigan was Bill Yearby, a big, fast tackle out of old Eastern High in Detroit. Some of the alumni had seen him play and said, 'If that kid comes to Michigan, we can win the Big Ten.'

"So we went to Fritz, who was athletics director then, and he finally gave us the okay to talk to Yearby. Up until then, I don't think a Michigan head coach even met any of the kids until they actually showed up for practice. Sure enough, Yearby anchored the defense that took us to the Rose Bowl in 1964 and Bump Elliot turned out to be a pretty good recruiter. But Bo was the master. He said that it was the part of his job that he hated, that it made him feel like a pimp. But he was the master."

Dave Rentschler
former M Club president, 1978–79

"I grew up in Massillon and if you know Massillon you know how deep the ties run with Ohio State. It's understood if you excel with Massillon, that's where you go to college. That's just the way it is.

"So Woody was around a lot. They were recruiting me heavily and I would have been a good fit with their system. But, you know, Woody was almost like a god in Ohio. You stood in awe of him. Bo just seemed more approachable to me, someone you could talk to, down to earth. He didn't come around as often but I felt like I knew him better. So I signed with Michigan."

Dennis Franklin
quarterback, 1974

"I was being recruited by both Michigan and Ohio State when I was playing at Washington High in Massillon. But my dad put it to me real clearly. 'If you go to Michigan,' he said, 'you'll be a traitor. I didn't raise my son to be a traitor.'

"So I had to tell Bo 'No, thanks.'"

Chris Spielman
Ohio State linebacker, 1987

"I'd heard two things when I was being recruited. I heard Woody didn't like to recruit kids who were from Columbus, because if they didn't play all kinds of people were in his ear. I also heard that he really didn't start to recruit you seriously until he knew that Bo was interested.

"Bo was interested and I was seriously considering going to Michigan. In fact, I was honored. In the end, I stayed in Columbus because I wanted my folks to see me play every week."

Archie Griffin
Ohio State two-time
Heisman Trophy winner,1975

"I was leaning toward UCLA my senior year at Kettering High in Detroit. My mom was pressuring me to stay home, but I liked the idea of going to school out in California.

"But Bo was scheduled for a home visit and he called ahead and asked my mom to prepare his favorite meal. I

Bo was seemingly able to cast a spell on local high-school stars like Detroit native Stan Edwards, who could have played in the Pac-10, and convince them to play for the Wolverines.

forget what it was, but she was only too happy to do it. He walked in the house, loosened up his tie, unbuttoned the top button on his shirt, rolled up his sleeves, and sat down at the table like he'd been doing it for the last 100 years.

"Then in his own fiery manner, he said, 'Mrs. Edwards, your son is going to get the best education money can buy. He is going to play in front of more people than anybody else in college football on every Saturday. And what's more he's going to be doing that 30 minutes away from this house.'

"What more did he have to say? Good-bye, UCLA."

Stan Edwards
running back, 1981

"I was pretty sure I'd be going to Michigan, but I really wanted to keep my options open. So I agreed to a campus visit to Arizona.

"I loved it there. Growing up in a city like Flint, the idea of warm winters was really appealing. It was a beautiful campus, pretty girls. I was convinced.

"I got home and told my dad that's where I was going. 'Oh, no you're not,' he said. We had a huge argument that ended with me stomping upstairs to my room and slamming the door shut. This was my decision, and no one was going to make up my mind for me.

"I was up there for an hour or two and all of a sudden I hear a Bam! Bam! on the door. I figure it's my dad wanting to continue the argument and I kind of growl at the door to come in. It swings open and in walks Bo.

"'What's this crap I hear about you going to Arizona?' he says. Then he lit into me for making such a stupid decision. He outlined again all the plusses of going to Michigan, but he could see I still wasn't 100 percent sure.

"'Listen to me, Leach,' he says. 'We play Arizona in a couple of years and when we do I'll tell my guys to kill you.'

"That convinced me."

Rick Leach
quarterback, 1978

Bo had no qualms about being blunt when recruiting Rick Leach and convincing him to attend Michigan instead of Arizona.

"Michigan didn't recruit too much in Florida back then, but Bo came down to Riviera Beach and really made an impression on my family. So I chose Michigan.

"But I'd never been that far away from home and after a few days there I got homesick. So I got on a plane after the first practice and went back to Florida. Bo figured out what happened and called down there and asked to speak to my grandmother. Whatever he said to her she just drove me right back out to the airport and put me on a plane back to Michigan. He told me later that I just needed some positive reinforcement.

"I heard him do some screaming but he never screamed at me. In fact, it was a great pleasure to play for Bo."

Anthony Carter
wide receiver, 1982

Carter was given uniform jersey No. 1 by Bo and from that time on it has been worn only by wide receivers deemed worthy by the coaching staff. But it was not a special honor handed out to his sensational freshman in 1979.

The number, indeed, had not been worn for 49 years after All-American and future coach Harry Kipke put it on in 1923. But in 1973, Bo gave it to defensive back Dave Whiteford. He wore it for three seasons, in only one of which he lettered. Then it was inherited by kicker Greg Willner for three years.

So there was no special cache to the jersey…until Bo gave it one by placing it at Carter's locker.

"Bo didn't come to Florida to recruit me. I made my visit up there, instead, which was one big reason I chose Miami. I was really sold on Michigan. The record of success and the Hall of Fame coach and all, and Bo was really impressive. It was freezing up there, snow everywhere. He kept telling me with my talent I was good enough to play in all kinds of weather. It won't be a problem.

"Then I walked into that stadium and they had my name spelled out on the scoreboard. Wow! That was cool. I could just see those 100,000 fans packed in there. That was a big selling point, along with the aura of Bo Schembechler.

"But then I went back home and Howard Schnellenberger, the new coach at Miami, said we would win a national championship down there and I could be warm and close to home, too. So I stayed there."

Bennie Blades
University of Miami safety, 1987

"When I heard that Bo was actually coming to my house, I was pretty damn shocked. I was being recruited by several schools, but I grew up outside of Detroit, in Southgate, and this was a pretty big deal. He was right there in my family's living room and I was blown away. In fact, the only people who were more excited than me were my parents.

"This was toward the end of his coaching career at Michigan and he was already some kind of legend. More than that, he had the ability to walk into a room and pretty much take it over. If any young player ever says that he wasn't intimidated by his presence, I'd have to say he was lying. But he made it very clear there weren't any stars on the Michigan team. The program was the star and it didn't make any difference if you were a walk-on from Topeka or a high school All-American from Massillon or a kid from Southgate.

"My only regret is that my son will not have the opportunity to play for him."

Keith Mitchell
tight end, 1988

"I had just come back from Vietnam in 1971 and enrolled in Michigan to complete my education. I'd played some football at Oxford High, north of Detroit, but no one had ever recruited me.

"A lot of the friends that I made in the dorm were football players and they encouraged me to come to some workouts with them at Crisler Arena. They were supposed to be for players only, but the coaches were all out recruiting and no one was checking up too closely, so I just kept going.

"One day I look up and Bo is standing there. He catches my eye and he kind of motions me over. 'Don't you think that if you wanted to go out for Michigan football you might check with a coach first?' he asked.

"He wasn't being unfriendly, just kind of curious. Like, 'Who is this guy?' He could have just sent me away. A lot of coaches would have done that. Instead, we started talking and he found out about my background in the military. Bo loved telling stories about the military and the next thing I know I'm in his office and we're telling war stories.

"I guess he figured out that I had the heart and the talent to fit into his system, and I lettered for the next three years."

Mike Lantry
place-kicker, 1974

"I'd been recruited by some Mid-America Conference schools when I was in high school. But my grades weren't up to par so I went into the military for three years.

"When I came out I got accepted to Michigan as a student, but in my own mind I felt I had something else to prove to myself. So I went to Lloyd Carr's office—he was an assistant coach then—and told him I'd like to go out for the team as a walk-on. I didn't know it but he'd asked Bo to come by and he sized me up with a few well-chosen words.

"Bo loved guys with a military background and when it turned out that we had served in the same unit, I was in. He always called me 'Sarge.' I stayed for three years and I was definitely not one of the marquee guys. But Bo made everyone on the scout team feel that they were integral to the team's success and when I got the Rookie of the Week award in practice before the Northwestern game it was a tremendous feeling."

Jim Sinclair
fullback, 1989

"I was a soccer player in high school, in Warren, outside of Detroit, and I played some basketball, too. I didn't even go out for football as a place-kicker until my senior year. I was offered a soccer scholarship at Oakland University, but I got it into my head that I wanted to make the Michigan team. So I scheduled a campus visit.

"I was on the field, making some kicks, and the next thing I know Bo is standing next to me. He starts right in asking me questions. 'Do you have good grades? Why do you want to play football at Michigan? What do you want to do with your life?'

"Then he motions to his coordinator and they sign me up right then and there. I almost died on the spot. I was in awe because I really didn't even consider myself a football player. This was just something I had to try for myself because I was such a diehard fan. The last thing I ever expected was that I could actually make that team. But Bo never missed a thing. I think he saw qualities in kids that other coaches missed.

"I had a back injury and really didn't even get a chance to play at Michigan until my senior year. People ask me, 'Don't you wish you'd have gone somewhere else so you could have played more?' Absolutely not. I got all the benefits of being part of one of the greatest college programs in history and made some of the closest friends in my life."

Mike Melnyk
place-kicker, 1984

"Growing up in Indiana, I was a huge Notre Dame fan. I agreed to a campus visit at Michigan for one big reason. Notre Dame wasn't recruiting me.

"On my last day in Ann Arbor I was called into Bo's office. I had no idea what he was going to ask me and so I couldn't prepare any answers. He just watched me walk across his office to the chair in front of his desk.

"As soon as I sat down, he said, 'Dixon, are you a Michigan man?' I said, 'Yes, sir. I am.' I still don't know why I said that. I'd never paid much attention to Michigan and really didn't know that much about Bo, either.

"But that was it, the entire interview. Years later when he wouldn't let Bill Frieder coach Michigan in the NCAA Tournament, and said 'Michigan will be coached by a Michigan man' I thought back to my interview. Those two words covered the world for Bo.

"I've got to admit, though, one of the biggest thrills of my college career was running out of the tunnel for the first time at Notre Dame. As things worked out, it's also where I got my law degree. So I had the best of both worlds."

Tom Dixon
center, 1983

"I was headed for Stanford. They'd recruited me and, of course, it is a great school academically. But I had always rooted for Michigan and I was watching them play in the Rose Bowl before making my commitment when it suddenly dawned on me that I had a chance to play for the team I was cheering for.

"So when I had my interview with Bo, I wanted to play for him but I also knew that if it didn't work out there was always Stanford, which isn't a bad fallback plan. So I came across as an adult instead of a nervous teenager, and I found out later that's what he liked about me. I was part of the last class he ever recruited and we got off on the right foot.

"I showed up for the first team meeting and I figured this was going to be nice and friendly. We'd just won the Rose Bowl and I thought it would be 'Let's get going, we're going to have a great season, rah rah rah.'

"He started off, instead, by listing five bars near campus he didn't want us going into and if we did we were off the team. That was just for openers. Then he went into a lecture about earrings and tattoos. Then he went into a rant, screaming at one of the stars because he hadn't worked on conditioning during the summer to prepare himself for this season. That was an eye-opener and for just a few minutes I wondered if I should have chosen Stanford. Not for long, but it crossed my mind."

Marc Milia
center, 1993

"Other recruiters promised me all kinds of things. You get suspicious after listening to too much of that. All Bo ever said was that he'd give me a fair chance. That was the most honest thing any recruiter had ever said to me. I knew then he wouldn't lie and play games with me."

Erick Anderson
linebacker, 1991

"He always said it didn't matter how you get to Michigan. Whether you were being recruited by everybody or whether you were a walk-on. Everyone would be treated the same. Other coaches may say that. But Bo meant it.

"I was the lowliest of the low, a walk-on from Grosse Pointe who only managed to get noticed because my Little

League coach was Dave Rentschler, who had a close, friendly relationship with Bo.

"He watched all the workouts and everything we did was measured and rated, no matter who we were. Once he said to me, 'I knew you would be good. I'm glad you're here.' I left the field walking on air. And I was on the demo team then.

"Only three walk-ons from my class made it all the way through. My roomie quit after two weeks. Too tough. But I thought that even if I never played a down, how could you have another experience like this?"

Karl Tech
special teams, 1981

"We finished our interview and Bo said that if he had a scholarship available I would get it. Then he stopped and looked into my eyes. I wanted to play there so badly and I guess that's what he saw. Because he offered me the scholarship right then and there."

Jamie Morris
running back, 1987

"I was coaching at a Cleveland-area high school and every year a Michigan recruiter paid us a visit. I hit it off with Gary Moeller, and he invited me to come up to their spring practice 'and we'll teach you some football.'

"Well, I must have gone up there 10 straight times and Bo was always so gracious. He'd let me sit in at staff meetings with his coaches and they'd be getting on each other, laughing and joking, and then when they left his office it was all business. What a great atmosphere he created. It might have helped that I went to Miami, just like he did, because he was usually very strict and tight about these things.

"The thing I always remember is getting a call from him about a player he had recruited from our school. 'Priefer,' he said, 'you get this guy on the phone and you tell him he had better start going to class or I am going to kick his ass.' I made that call. I was afraid not to make that call.

"I don't have a lot of regrets about my career. I've been very blessed. But the one regret I do have is that I never had the opportunity to work with him. I thought to me that would have been one of the great things in my life."

Chuck Priefer
Detroit Lions special teams coach,
1997–2006

"Bo was a very complex individual, almost two men in the same body. When the kids got here the first year they were scared to death of him. The second year they hated him. The third year they started to say, 'Well, he's not as bad as I thought.' By the time they graduated they had a love affair with Bo."

Jerry Hanlon
assistant coach, 1969–91

"I played my first game at Michigan seven years after Bo coached his last one. But he played a big part in my recruiting process.

"I pretty much knew where I was going the whole time, but I didn't tell the Michigan coaches that. So I was in Ann Arbor on my official visit and Coach Carr sticks my dad and me in Coach Schembechler's office for an hour and a half.

"It was just the three of us talking, mostly Bo telling stories, entertaining my dad and me. He was getting us motivated, fired up so that I'd come to Michigan. The whole time I'm looking at my dad and thinking, 'I don't have to be sold. I'm already coming here.'

"But if there were any doubts, all I had to do was look at my dad's face while Bo was talking and they were gone. It was the most memorable recruiting visit I had."

Jeff Backus
offensive lineman, 2000

CHAPTER
5

Soul and Inspiration

Bo downplayed the effect of his pregame speeches, but he said he always regretted the one motivational speech he never gave.

"We went into the 1980 season with what I thought was one of my best teams at Michigan," he said. "But we lost our second game at Notre Dame and then we came home and got beaten by South Carolina. At that point, I knew something was wrong but I couldn't tell what it was.

"My assistants came to me and said they were getting a lot of complaints from the players. The practices were too long. The coaches were too critical. There was too much hitting.

"I couldn't believe my ears. So I called in one of my captains, Andy Cannavino, to hear what he had to say about this. 'It's true,' he said. 'Football just isn't fun anymore.'

"Well, I went through the roof and reminded him of a few things. The fact that his father had played at Ohio State but they did not offer him a scholarship, for one. The fact that being elected captain carries with it certain responsibilities, for another.

"'And you have the audacity to stand there and tell me that *we* are the problem,' I said. 'The only problem with this team is you.'

"He never said a word. But I want to tell you for the rest of that season Andy Cannavino was the greatest captain I ever had.

We won every other game; the last four weeks of the season nobody crossed our goal line and then we beat Washington in the Rose Bowl.

"But those two losses, in my mind, cost us a national championship, and that's on me. It was my fault. I should have seen

Bo was a master at motivation and was always in command of his team.

what was happening and had that conversation before it had ever reached that stage.

"The head coach failed to do his job. I did not create the positive attitude before the season began. I never made that mistake again. I always, always coached attitude first.

"If you go into the team meeting room today you'll see a sign that says: 'Blame no one. Expect nothing. Do something.' That is attitude."

"I heard him give a speech at Crisler Arena and was introduced to him right afterward. All I could think of was how incredible it must be to play for this man and listen to him on a daily basis. It was extremely motivational.

"He walked away and I was ready to run my events right then and there. I think there must have been an after-effect because I went on to take a second in the regional meet and an eighth in the NCAAs. So here was someone else he inspired to go beyond herself."

Mindy Rowand-Schmidt
track, 1990

"While he was exercising at the Matt Mann Pool he became infuriated that swimmers from other schools held the pool records there. Once he actually shook a finger in my face and told me that I had to get Mark Spitz's name off the board in the 200-yard butterfly; especially since he had been swimming for our archrival, Indiana.

"I was too scared to tell him that it wasn't my event. I just nodded and agreed and hurried back to the locker room.

Tom Szuba
swimming, 1976

"He used to say to me, 'James, you have the worst body in the history of Michigan football.' Being a smart-ass, I'd answer back, 'If it's so bad how come I play so much?' Bo would say, 'Because I'm a helluva coach.'

"It was all part of the process, trying to goad you into getting more out of yourself. I enjoyed our little exchanges, though.

"He would poke me in the chest and say, 'James, you're not half the tackle I was.' And I'd say, 'That's because you played for a better coach than I did.' Bo laughed louder than anybody.

"We were supposed to have a pretty good team in 1983 and the second game we got beaten by Washington. Bo came into the locker room the next practice and he was fuming. He said, 'The papers are saying we were *man*-handled by Washington. How do we tell guys like [Dan] Dierdorf and [Reggie] McKenzie that we've been *man*-handled? Can you imagine anyone *man*-handling those Michigan teams?

"Needless to add, we went out and took care of Wisconsin the next week."

Doug James
offensive lineman, 1984

"We knew that sometime during the week of a big game, we'd get a call from Bo. The practice field wasn't too far from the Band Building and we'd be told at a given time to come marching over to the field, surround the players, and play 'The Victors.'

"All the players would sing and Bo would always say, 'That's the greatest fight song ever written.' Oh, it was a helluva scene. That's Michigan tradition and he played on it masterfully."

George Cavender
former Michigan band director, 1971–79

"Bo knew how to use that Michigan tradition. Do you know how many kids said they came to Michigan because of the helmet? People laugh, but that's not something to laugh about. That helmet stands for something. It stands for uniqueness. It stands for all the things carried on by Michigan teams over the years.

"People come to expect certain things. They grow comfortable with it. That's what he understood."

Jerry Hanlon
assistant coach, 1969–91

According to longtime assistant Jerry Hanlon, Bo believed deeply in and knew how to use Michigan's rich football tradition to drive his team to success.

"Bo made me feel that I owed it to every man, woman, and child in the state of Michigan to run hard. I felt that way because Bo kept screaming it in our faces. It was one of his greatest pregame speeches, really over the top. We ate it up. At the very least, it got my attention.

"After he gave one of these speeches, all I wanted to do was make him say 'Wow.' I didn't care what anybody else thought, just him. In my mind, that was the definition of success. He knew it, too, and that's the button he kept pushing.

"He made me earn my stripes every Saturday by saying things like, 'I don't think you can gain 100 yards against this defense today. I don't think you've got it in you.'

"If I messed up, he'd say, 'Morris, you are the last 5'7" tailback I will ever recruit.' I hated when he yelled at me, but it drove me. Of course, I wasn't crazy about it when he called me 'the cutest little running back in America' either. He was just a magician when it came to motivation and handling people."

Jamie Morris
running back, 1987

"Most of his motivational speeches involved a lot of yelling. They ran together after a while, but when you came right down to it they always focused on execution and turnovers. If he needed to call out an individual player, he did it, too."

Dennis Franklin
quarterback, 1974

"The real pregame speech always came on Thursday. He would get so fired up and emotional that you'd be ready to tear your desk up, and it carried all the way through to Saturday. When the dust settled and you saw this old guy in glasses standing there, you'd run through the wall for him.

"I've seen videotapes of Bo giving one of these speeches, but it doesn't begin to capture the emotion of what it was like to actually be in that room."

Doug Daugherty
offensive lineman, 1989

Doug Daugherty was moved by Bo's speeches.

"His one motivational saying that he constantly drilled into us was 'You get better or you get worse every day. You never stay the same.' That and his other favorite saying, 'Nothing good ever happens after midnight.'

"After a while, I understood that a lot of his performances were part of an act. He knew his responsibility and it was the role he had to play as a head coach. If he needed to be an actor, he acted."

Fritz Seyferth
running back, 1971

"We came into the 1981 season as favorites to win the Big 10 and a possible national title. Then we lost to Wisconsin in the opener and Bo went wild. His practices were always intense, but these were the worst of all.

"He felt we had lost because of a breakdown in open-field tackling by the defensive backfield. I was on the demo team and my assignment was to beat the starters in this drill.

"Needless to say, they were loaded for bear and during the drill I broke my arm. Bo visited the hospital and told me to hang in there and I'd be back with the team. Next week we smashed Notre Dame and I was in the locker room after the game. In front of the entire team, he gave me the scout team Player of the Week award. That was the greatest memory."

John Ferens
defensive back, 1983

"The fourth game of the 1977 season, we played Texas A&M. We were ranked number three in the country and they were fifth, and they were going on about how they were going to come into our stadium and give us a Texas-sized whupping. They were going to show us how to play physical Southwest Conference–style football.

"That's all Bo had to hear. He came into the meeting room on Tuesday and chucked the newspaper on the floor, grabbed the podium and threw it against the wall. That kind of got everyone's attention.

"Then he looked at the team and said, 'I don't care if we win or lose, boys.' He was breathing hard, almost panting. 'But no Texas team is ever going to come into this stadium and outhit us. We may lose but they will *not* outhit us. Understand that!'

"We never had practices with that kind of intensity. But at the half we were behind 3–0. I was scared to death going into that locker room. I thought he was going to kill us.

"Instead, he was rubbing his hands together and smiling. 'All right, guys,' he said. 'We've got 'em figured out now. We're going back out there and we're gonna do this, that, and the other and we're gonna get 'em.' He was just as happy as he could be.

"Final score: Michigan 41, Texas A&M 3. Enough said."

Stan Edwards
running back, 1981

"The motivational speeches didn't stop with the team. I came home from school at Miami University for the Thanksgiving holiday in 1989. Dad didn't like my haircut. He demanded that I get it trimmed.

"Next day I went to the barber and had him cut the hair on the sides of my head and leave the middle part long. Dad was absolutely baffled and asked me what in the world was I thinking wearing my hair that way.

"I told him that's how my girlfriend liked it. He just looked at me and said, 'Girlfriend? You mean ex-girlfriend.' Then he went into a whole birds and bees sort of thing and told me that when I was more worldly I'd understand more about girls."

Shemy Schembechler
Bo's youngest son

"When Bo joined the Detroit Tigers as president, many baseball people doubted that he could be a successful executive. They didn't think the techniques he used in college football could work in professional sports.

"His first day in spring training, with about 150 veteran players, rookies, and coaches gathered around him, he went into a speech that just had them all spellbound; even the Spanish-speaking players who didn't understand a word he was saying.

"They seemed captivated by a man whose presence transcended all sports.

"People were arguing at the time that it was a bad move for the Tigers because how much did Bo really know about baseball? But that missed the whole point. He wasn't brought in to manage ballgames. His job was to manage people, and he was very good at that."

Joe McDonald
former Tigers executive, 1987–92

"I traveled with him to Ottawa, in Canada, one time when he was appearing at a tribute for Jim Coode. He was a teammate of mine and had played offensive tackle for Bo in the early '70s.

"But he had come down with Lou Gehrig's disease and people were pouring in to tell them how much he meant to them and doing honor to his life. He died shortly after this benefit.

"Bo gave one of his greatest speeches that night. Remember this was in Canada where people don't know all that much about American college football and its coaches. But he connected with that audience and just held them rapt. He could connect with anybody."

Bob Thornbladh
fullback, 1973

"Before the Notre Dame game one year, a defensive lineman came into the meeting room wearing a Notre Dame T-shirt. Bo took one look and just started yelling at the guy. 'Get out of here with that shirt on.' He just flipped out on the poor guy and when he tried to say something Bo wasn't having any of it. He threw him right out of the room.

"His position coach went out in the hallway after him and a few minutes later he came back in, walked over to Bo, and started whispering in his ear. Bo is looking straight ahead and starts nodding his head as if he understands.

"So the coach comes back in with the player and now Bo can see that he had written the word "sucks" in black marker under the Notre Dame on his shirt. That's why he was wearing it. He sat back down and the meeting went on with not another word said about it."

Mike Melnyk
place-kicker, 1984

"I've known people who could lead you as a disciplinarian and I've known people who could lead you as a father. Bo was the only person I ever saw who could do both.

"I remember misreading the center's block in a practice before the Notre Dame game one year and screwed up the play. He came up to me and said, 'Sarge, you've just laid the biggest egg I've ever seen in this program.'

"He put me on the traveling squad to the 1989 Rose Bowl even though I was getting married a month later. He knew it, too. So just to make sure I'd keep my mind on the business at hand, he kept saying, 'I should have never taken you here. Prove to me I'm wrong.'"

Jim Sinclair
fullback, 1988

"The Michigan State game always came in for special treatment. Bo pushed us before that one because he wanted to stomp them and leave no doubt about which was the dominant program in the state. He regarded that game as a showcase, one of the biggest recruiting tools he had available to him.

"I think it was also payback for State's vote for Ohio State after the 1973 season. That kept Michigan out of the Rose

Bowl after they had played OSU to a 10–10 tie. He never forgave them for voting that way."

Tom Dixon
center, 1983

"He was a great motivator but he hated it when someone turned the tables on him. We were playing Iowa in 1981 and it was the first time Bo was coaching against Hayden Fry. Iowa hadn't beaten Michigan in almost 20 years and Fry had his team all jacked up coming into Ann Arbor. They beat us 9–7.

"Bo took it personally because Hayden had beaten him at his own game. Next year we went into Iowa City and he gave a speech. He said that all 22 players had to beat the man in front of them and we would win. Then we could lift Bo on our shoulders, carry him over to the Iowa sideline, and he'd punch Hayden Fry right in the mouth.

"We won big, but Bo didn't follow through on his part of the deal."

Paul Girgash
linebacker, 1983

"Hayden Fry painted the visitors' locker room pink at the Iowa stadium before the 1985 Michigan game. He'd read somewhere that the color made people passive.

"I think Bo was amused at first. He thought he could out-motivate any color there was. But Iowa won that game and three years later when Michigan went in there again, they played us to a tie.

"That did it. In 1989 before we went back to Iowa City, Bo ordered the equipment managers to buy white butcher paper and go into that locker room and cover every square inch of the wall. We won the game, 26–12, and Bo just left all the white paper up there when we left."

Doug Daugherty
offensive lineman, 1989

"My freshman year was 1979. At the full team meeting after we'd lost to Notre Dame in the second game of the season, Bo came into the room, walked to the blackboard, and wrote 'October 4, 1975.'

"We didn't know what that meant and he just stood there and let us look at that date. Then he explained. This was the first time Michigan hadn't been ranked in the top 10 since that date. Not just in the polls, but in the top 10. We'd fallen to number 11. That's when I learned that when you played for Bo Schembechler it wasn't enough to be good. Only greatness would suffice.

"I loved the way he answered a question that might deserve a simple 'yes' with 'affirmative!' I loved the Saturday morning meetings at the hotel. Bo would always end them by shouting: 'Do I have 11? All I need is 11.' Then he would lead us out the door to the bus.

"I loved how Bo always pitted us against everybody else. Especially the media, most of whom, he said, had never even worn a jock strap—although his language was a lot more colorful than that."

Craig Dunaway
tight end, 1982, and
M Club president, 2006–07

"Bo had lost five straight Rose Bowls when we went out to play Washington after the 1980 season. He said, 'Just get me a lead at the half. Every one of those games we lost, we were behind at the half. Just get me the lead, even if it's one point.'

"That's exactly what it was. We were ahead 7–6 at the half and not playing well. I hadn't gone to our great All-American receiver Anthony Carter at all. He hadn't caught a single pass. He was being well covered and I felt that I'd be forcing it.

"At halftime, he said, 'Force it.' Anthony caught five passes and scored a touchdown. And the defense never gave up another point."

John Wangler
quarterback, 1980

CHAPTER
6

Loyalty

"He thought of himself as a cross between chief executive officer of the corporation of Michigan football and the patriarch of a family. He was always demanding, but at the same time he took an interest in you and remembered the small details of everyone's life and family.

"In my junior year—that was 1980—he asked me to sacrifice my statistics and move from tailback to be a blocking fullback for Butch Woolfolk and Lawrence Ricks. Bo was very concerned that I would resent the move because it might hurt my prospects of getting drafted by the pros.

"I had started seven games at tailback in '79. But Butch had been coming on and I could see that. I knew that I wouldn't be getting the ball that much anymore but I sincerely wanted to help the team any way I could.

"Bo told me numerous times after that how much he respected me for going that route. I think it made us a little closer than he was to other members of the team when I was still playing. And as it turned out I was drafted by Houston when I came out of school and spent five years as a back in the pros."

Stan Edwards
back, 1981

By almost all counts, Bo was kind-hearted once he got to know you and was loyal to a fault to anyone who was part of his Michigan family.

"He would do whatever he could for his players, but it had to be strictly within the rules. There was no wiggle room on that issue. Not one inch.

"He tried to get summer jobs for as many of his players as possible. He found out that one of his stars was getting paid $13 an hour, and everyone else on the job was only making $12. He went to the employer and demanded to know whether his guy was getting the extra buck because he was bringing some special skill to the job or because he was a Michigan football player.

"When the answer didn't satisfy him he demanded that the kid's pay be knocked down to $12, same as everyone else's. His ears were always open to stuff like that. The rules were the rules, and even if he may have disagreed with some of the rules he felt that if you didn't stay within them you didn't deserve to win."

Dave Rentschler
former M Club president, 1978–79

"There was a point where I almost quit the team and left school. It was my sophomore year. We finished the 1986 regular season with a trip to play at Hawaii and when I got home I was told my dad had gone missing. No one knew where he was or even if he was still alive.

"My mom and two young sisters were still at home and I felt that I had to be there for them. I made all the arrangements and was literally one hour away from moving back home.

"Lloyd Carr, who was an assistant coach then, heard that I was leaving and he came up to me and said, 'Bo is pissed and wants to see you.' He marched me right into Bo's office. He basically walked over, sat down next to me, looked me straight in the eye, and said, 'You are not quitting.'

"He knew everything that was going on. He also knew how hard I had worked that season, in school and on the team, and he was not going to let me throw it away. He then proceeded to walk me through the toughest time in my life.

"I was so down. I'd just be sitting in class staring at the floor, wondering where my father was. Bo wouldn't let me get away with holding a self-pity party. I was losing a year out of my life and he wouldn't let me do it. He kept asking what he could do for my mother and my sisters and for me. 'There is no quitting in life, son,' he said.

"I had lost a father but this man standing in front of me was every bit my father. I knew I was safe and I cried right in front of him.

"When he pulled me aside next season and told me how proud he was of me, it was the greatest moment of my life. I was so proud to be out on the field when he won his 200th game and to help him beat USC in the Rose Bowl as a senior. That man saved my life."

Keith Mitchell
end, 1988

"Every Michigan athletic team was important to Bo. My first year as head coach of the wrestling team we lost to Iowa, which was the number one ranked team in the country.

"He was standing on a balcony when I walked into the athletic department offices and he yelled down to me: 'What in hell are you doing losing to Iowa?'

"They may have been a doormat in football back then but he didn't know they were a powerhouse in wrestling. Or maybe he did and was just getting in the needle. Anyhow, I answered back, 'What in hell are you doing losing to Ohio State?'

He laughed and invited me up to his office for a chat and we were close friends from then on."

Bill Johannesen
wrestling coach, 1974–78

Keith Mitchell remembers how compassionate Bo was when he learned of Mitchell's family loss.

"The first time I met him I needed to go over the plans for our banquet at which he was going to speak. I walked into his office and I was wearing a Michigan State shirt from my playing days.

"'What are you wearing?' he growled at me. 'Why are you wearing that?' He scared the daylights out of me. Then at the banquet he brought out a Michigan sweatsuit and presented it to me, the first one I'd ever owned.

"A little while after we had won the NCAA softball tournament, I was eating at a restaurant on Main Street and I looked up and there was Bo waiting on the sidewalk to catch my eye. He just wanted to congratulate me and tell me how proud he was of the team. When any Michigan team accomplished something it meant everything to him.

"I remember the last time I saw him, too, in the parking lot near Schembechler Hall. I asked him how he was feeling and he said, 'Ah, it would have felled a lesser man.'"

Carol Hutchins
Michigan softball coach

"Bo demanded loyalty but he also had limits. Midway through the 1989 season, Tony Boles was running wild for Michigan. He'd just rushed for 158 yards against Indiana and there was Heisman talk. At his Monday luncheon he was asked if he would campaign to get Boles the award and Bo exploded.

"'That's not my job. If you like him, you vote for him. But I'm not going to sit up here and tell you how great he is.'

"Bo knew he had another back, Leroy Hoard, who was just as good. He knew individual awards do not help team goals. And he knew Boles was struggling academically and a Heisman campaign could hinder his schoolwork."

Bob Wojnowski
Detroit News columnist

"It was very unusual for him to give out individual praise, and we all knew that. But at the end of my senior season, Bo called me 'the best football player in the United States of America' and said that if I didn't win the Heisman he'd be very much surprised.

"Well, I didn't get the Heisman, but I did pick up a few other Player of the Year awards. And it was nice to hear what Bo thought of me.

"Before the Notre Dame game that year, I'd sprained my ankle real badly in practice. They were getting my backup, B.J. Dickey, ready to start and when I missed the Tuesday and Wednesday scrimmages I was sure he wouldn't let me start the game. That was a hard-and-fast rule when you played for Bo.

"On Friday, though, I took part in some drills and he made the decision to go with me. The very first play from scrimmage, I messed up a handoff to our running back, Russell Davis, and Notre Dame recovered the fumble and drove right in for a touchdown. The rest of the first half I wasn't much better and we were down 14–7.

"We went into the locker room and he pushed me up against a locker and told me to get my act together. Man, I forgot all about the ankle when I went back on the field. I threw three touchdown passes and beat Joe Montana, 28–14.

"But the real high point came when Bo said afterward that it wasn't my best running and passing performance. 'But guts wise...oh, yeah.'

"I never missed a game with an injury, even though I got knocked silly with a forearm to the head against Oklahoma in the Orange Bowl my freshman year. It only took me out of the third quarter, though."

Rick Leach
quarterback, 1978

"I was driving along Interstate 94 one night and here's this poor guy trying to hitch a ride along the side of the highway. He was just caked in snow and ice. I did a double take and it's Bo. His car had stalled.

"I backed up and he got in and started to complain. 'You know, while I was standing there three police cars passed me by.' 'Well, Bo,' I told him. 'You did go 6–6 last year.'"

Jon Falk
Michigan football equipment manager

"The man was totally honest with his players. His office door was never closed. To me that meant two things. You could walk in there anytime, and nothing would ever be said that couldn't be said with the door wide open."

Erick Anderson
linebacker, 1992

"He knew how much playing for Michigan meant to me and how hard I worked. On the last carry I ever had at

Michigan Stadium he called my number with two minutes
to play so that I got to score the winning touchdown
against Ohio State in 1971. That was his reward to me. Of
course, he also knew that nothing was going to stop me
from getting into the end zone."

Billy Taylor
running back, 1971

In the book *Man in Motion*, which Bo wrote with the great
Detroit sports columnist Joe Falls, he recounted one of the
most difficult situations he ever encountered. Sophomore quarterback Tom Slade had led Michigan to an 11–1 record in 1971,
losing only to Stanford by one point. But it was one instance
where loyalty had its limits.

"The following year, Dennis Franklin was ready to play
as a sophomore and I had to start him. We had no
passing game at all with Tommy and he knew it. Before
the opening game with Northwestern I gave a written
exam to our quarterbacks, asking them about game
situations, automatics, formations, that sort of thing. One
of the questions was: 'What can you do to beat
Northwestern?'

"This was Slade's answer: 'Show great enthusiasm. Be a
leader and encourage Denny and give him every show of
encouragement and confidence before, during, and after
the game. Be ready for any situation; the point after
touchdown, the field goal, injury to quarterbacks. Be
aware of what is going on on the field in case I do get to
play. Help Mike Lantry by trying to relax him and keep him
as cool as possible. Catch the ball and place it perfectly on
the tee. Be alert and be sharp.'

"And that was from a kid who had just lost his job to a younger player. That was magnificent."

Bo Schembechler
Man in Motion

"In his autobiography, Bo called me the cockiest quarterback he ever had at Michigan. I took that as a compliment.

"There was one practice where I started chewing out receivers for failing to run their deep routes properly. Jerry Hanlon told me later that Bo liked that and said, 'He can't stand people not being as competitive as he is.'

"But maybe I pushed it a little in 1986 when I was the offensive team captain. We lost to Minnesota on a last-second field goal the week before Ohio State. It ruined our unbeaten season and when we went into Columbus we were ranked number six and they were number seven. The game was for the Rose Bowl, as usual.

"Well, we were all distraught after the Minnesota game and I stood up and said, 'I guarantee we will beat Ohio State and go to Pasadena. I don't care if we play them in Columbus or in a parking lot or in an alley at midnight. We'll beat them.'

"Hanlon heard that and he was apoplectic. He said he wanted to kill me. All Bo did, though, was tell me, 'You better be right.' Then he told the media, 'I'd be more concerned if he didn't expect to win.'

"He didn't like giving the opposition any ammunition to use against us, and that's the last thing we needed against Ohio State because they hated us so much already. But Bo rallied the other coaches and players around me and said, 'The son of a gun made a statement and now we're going to have to back him up.'

"We won that game 26–24, and he stood by me all the way. My dad had been an assistant under Bo and I literally grew up around the Michigan program, which may be why I was cocky enough to say something like that."

Jim Harbaugh
quarterback, 1986

"After graduation we kept in touch, and when I was offered a job at the university I asked to come in to see him for some advice. I expected a five-minute talk. Instead he took me to breakfast and spent an hour going over my qualifications.

"I wasn't a four-year starter at Michigan. I was just one guy on the team. But he said to me, 'You're not just any guy applying for this job. You're a Michigan man.'

"He believed that you couldn't put a dollar sign on being able to say that. It meant everything."

Doug Daugherty
offensive lineman, 1989

"After he retired, the softer side of his personality came out. Oh, he was still stubborn and argumentative. That didn't change. But he could be in a meeting and his secretary could come in and say, 'The president of the university is on the phone,' and he'd say, 'Tell him I'll call back later.' I believe he'd have said the same thing if it was the president of the United States.

"But let one of his former players call and say that he needed to see Bo. Boom. He'd drop everything and leave immediately to see him. He had a soft spot for every kid who ever played for him, and his loyalty to them was boundless."

Jerry Hanlon
assistant coach, 1969–91

"There were strict limits on the size of Big Ten traveling squads when Bo got to Michigan. You only got to take so many to the Rose Bowl. The others could come, too, but not as part of the team.

"He was infuriated by that. He felt every player on the demo team was just as integral to the team's success as the starters. He got that rule changed so they all could be on the field for that game. He felt he owed that to the players who did everything he asked them to.

"Same thing with the annual banquet in Detroit honoring the team. It was always supposed to be just for the lettermen. Other players weren't invited. My first year on the team, I didn't letter. All my friends on the team went to the banquet. I felt like Ann Arbor had emptied out and I was left all alone.

"I mentioned that to Bo and when it came time for the 1969 banquet he insisted that every member of his team had to be invited. If they weren't, he told the organizers, none of them would come. Well, they had to redo a lot of tables at the last minute, but Bo made it clear that it was either that or call off the banquet completely."

Dave Rentschler
former M Club president, 1978–79

CHAPTER 7

Conflicts

There were three major upheavals during Bo's tenure at Michigan: the aftermath of the 10–10 tie with Ohio State in 1973, the offer to coach Texas A&M in 1982, and the decision to name Steve Fisher as basketball coach at the start of the 1989 NCAA tournament when Bo was also acting as the athletics director.

Each of them defined what he understood as loyalty and playing by the rules.

"I broke my collarbone in the fourth quarter of that Ohio State game. It wasn't quite the same buildup that you had before the 2006 game, but it was close. We were both undefeated, and Ohio State was ranked number one. We were ranked fourth, although no one had come within two touchdowns of us all year.

"The game was in Ann Arbor and there were 105,000 people in the stands, a Michigan Stadium record at the time. They had us down 10–0 at the half, and then we started coming back on them.

"Mike Lantry kicked a field goal and I scored on a 10-yard run and it was tied with 10 minutes to play. We were moving again with two minutes left. I was running to my right and threw back to the left and Van Ness DeCree hit me high. As soon as I went down, I knew something was wrong. He landed on me kind of funny and I heard something pop. I went out of the game and they told me right away on the sidelines that the collarbone was broken.

"We couldn't move the ball after I had to go out. Mike had to try a long field goal and he missed. But we intercepted and with 24 seconds to play he tried another one, but it also missed. Well, we figured it would have been nice to win, but we knew a tie clinched the Rose Bowl trip.

"The Big 10 policy was that if there was a first-place tie, the team that hadn't been to the bowl for the longest time got the trip. Since OSU had gone the year before, we were in. We never dreamed that the Big 10 athletics directors would vote against us. That vote was supposed to be a formality. But the Big 10 had lost three straight Rose Bowls and the commissioner thought that with me out of the game, Michigan had no chance against Southern California. So there was a lot of lobbying going on, and on Sunday we were told that Ohio State had won the vote, 6–4.

"Bo was in a TV studio in downtown Detroit taping his weekly show and saying how much he was looking forward to the bowl game. When he came out, a sportswriter told him that the vote had gone the other way. He was just stunned. He just couldn't believe they would do anything that was so unfair.

"He spoke to the team on Monday and it was the first time any of us saw the emotional side of him. He was almost in tears. 'It's my fault, guys,' he said. 'You did everything I told you to do, paid your dues and it wasn't enough.'

Since Bo was a man of such strong beliefs, he wasn't afraid to brush up against officials, critics, or perceived injustices.

"It was the first time I realized he wasn't invincible. But for the first time it also made him seem more like a father figure than this hard-nosed coach.

"By the time the bowl game was played, my shoulder was fine. I even went out and threw some passes in the snow with the news photographers snapping away. I just wanted to make sure those Big Ten voters knew what a terrible decision they had made.

"That was a tremendous team and Bo always said we could have handled Southern Cal with my backup, Larry Cipa, at quarterback.

"I watched the game at my mom's house back in Massillon and it was the emptiest feeling I ever had in my life. I started at quarterback for three years, the team went 30–2–1, and we never went to a bowl game. Not one. In those years, it was the Rose Bowl or nothing in the Big Ten. It just wasn't right. In fact, it was a doggone crime."

Dennis Franklin
quarterback, 1974

Bo called that game "the greatest injustice in the history of college football" and it rankled him for the rest of his life. "We had a much better team than Ohio State," he said. "Woody came up to me afterward and said, 'Boy, we're going to have a good representative out there. Good luck, Bo. They're sending the right team.'

"Of course, the next day when the vote was announced," he said, "'I can understand them voting for us.'

"I was enraged. I wanted [Big Ten commissioner] Wayne Duke to come before my team and tell them they aren't good enough. I wanted him to tell Dennis Franklin that in his medical opinion he is not capable of playing against Southern Cal. I wanted him to look Larry Cipa in the eye and tell him he's not good enough to quarterback Michigan in the Rose Bowl.

"I vowed never to forget what happened. I told myself that if I ever let up on my bitterness over that decision then I wouldn't be doing justice to those players."

There was an eerie, almost forgotten echo of this incident, however. A very similar thing had occurred at Ohio State in 1961, when Bo was Woody's top assistant. The Buckeyes had

Because he believed in Michigan so deeply, it was painful for Bo whenever something negative happened to his beloved institution.

clobbered Michigan, 50–20, to win the Big Ten title and the trip to the Rose Bowl.

"We were at an alumni banquet in Cleveland," said Bo, "when we got word that the faculty board of control had voted to decline the bowl bid. It said that Woody's on-the-field success was jeopardizing our academic standing. So we stayed home and the runner-up, Minnesota, went out there for the second year in a row.

"I had never seen Woody so angry and the two of us just walked around downtown Cleveland for hours. Finally he decided to go ahead with his speech. 'These people who have voted this decision today,' he said, 'have never played in a Rose Bowl. They cannot comprehend the pride and the confidence and the lifelong memories that a game like this gives the young men who play college football.

"'To deny these young men this precious chance is the worst judgment they could possibly exercise.'"

Schembechler said it was the first time he had ever seen Woody cry; tears that would be repeated 12 years later when his own team was denied a Rose Bowl trip it had earned.

"He took it upon himself as a personal crusade to get the bowl restriction lifted by the Big Ten. Three of his other teams never went to a bowl, but Bo could accept that because they didn't finish first in the conference. When he did finish first and they still couldn't go, it was just too much. The rules were the rules and the Big Ten had broken faith. So he had no qualms about getting the rules changed.

"He always said that he had no control over a national championship. 'I won't bootlick to get a national ranking,' he said. He took undefeated teams into the Ohio State game every year between 1970 and 1975—six years in a row. And in not one of those games did Michigan go in ranked higher than third.

"Every team in the Big Ten owes Bo a big debt because that 10–10 tie and the injustice that followed led directly to the teams in the conference being eligible for other bowls. When I hear people wrote off some postseason games as a 'minor bowl' I think back to this incident and wonder how that team would have felt about playing in one of those games."

Dave Rentschler
former M Club president, 1978–79

"I missed those two field goals in the 1973 game. Then the next year we went down to Columbus and were behind 12–10 in the fourth quarter and I missed the field goal that would have won the game. It was my last kick for Michigan.

"Bo insisted right to the end that the kick was good. It went high and over the left upright. But he said the crowd would have mobbed the officials if they had called it good in Columbus.

"The stakes were so high. Getting to the Rose Bowl was our whole season. I know he was bitterly disappointed about what had happened the previous year and now we had just missed out again.

"I'll never know if that last field goal was good or not. But I do know Bo never let me get down on myself."

Mike Lantry
place-kicker, 1974

"The 1981 season wasn't a real great one—at least not by Michigan standards. The team finished the regular season with three conference losses and ended up going to the old Bluebonnet Bowl, at the Houston Astrodome. They beat UCLA there.

"When we got back to Detroit I happened to be on the phone with his wife, Millie. She was as much a part of his staff as the assistant coaches. If players that I had helped recruit ran into problems I could always go to Millie to get Bo's ear. When we needed a place for an M Club office for former letter winners, she even got Bo to put out a fund-raising challenge to alumni so we could refurbish a part of the University Golf Course clubhouse.

"So I spoke to her quite often. This conversation was about a fund-raiser, so she put him on the phone to hear my pitch. Bo listened for a minute or two and then said, 'Dave, don't go on. I'm not going to be the coach.'

"Stunned? That's putting it mildly. I didn't know what to say. Finally I managed to blurt out, 'I never thought you'd go to the pros.'

"'Who said anything about the pros?' he said. 'It's Texas A&M. They made the approach when we were down there for the bowl game.'

"Apparently, there was some big oil money behind this and they were using Gil Brandt, who was then head of player personnel for the Dallas Cowboys, as a go-between.

"I didn't know what to do. I just knew I couldn't allow this to happen. But the president of the university was stuck in a snowstorm in Washington, D.C., after attending a conference, and Don Canham was on vacation and unreachable by phone.

"It didn't make sense to me. Dollars did not sway Bo. The work was everything. He was making in the mid-80s a year, which wasn't bad money by the standards of the early 1980s. He thought he'd put the Texas people off by asking for $350,000, and to his shock they told him they would work it out.

"I rounded up Roger Zatkoff, who is a bulwark of the M Club and also was very close to Bo, and the two of us went over to his house to meet with him. He was obviously upset. He looked at us and said, 'Why do I have to go?' Millie was crying and gave me a hug. I just didn't understand what was going on.

"Then it came out. There had been a meeting of the faculty control committee and some remarks were made casting doubt on Bo's recruiting practices. They were especially critical of his recruiting Anthony Carter. They didn't think his grades and scores were up to Michigan standards and they implied that university admission rules must have been violated.

"Bo was wounded. He was scrupulous about recruiting and he only went after kids with character, the ones he felt could graduate with a little help. If they couldn't do that, he didn't want 'em. It was strictly by the rules.

"So I finally saw how to approach him. 'You go to the Southwest Conference and you know they cheat like crazy down there,' I told him. 'You won't be able to tolerate that.' Southern Methodist would get the 'death penalty' for repeated violations in a few more years.

"Then I said, 'You've already given Michigan your health and you've only got that to give once.'

"It was obvious to me that he wanted to stay, but that big offer was on the table and we thought he had to get some kind of enhanced package. So Fritz Seyferth, who was then associate athletics director, and Tom Monaghan, who owned Domino's Pizza, put together something that included Bo getting a Domino's franchise in Columbus, Ohio. We all thought that was a nice touch.

"Another thing happened during this period. A few years before, several of us had presented Bo with an M ring. He said at the time that once he put it on he would never take it off. But while the discussions were going on with A&M, he put the ring aside.

"Afterward, it never left his finger."

Dave Rentschler
former M Club president, 1978–79

"I interviewed Bo in 1996 for *BLITZ Magazine* as a Michigan alum and pretty diehard Wolverines fan. I had some real issues with Bo over the years, but I do think he was a man of integrity and that his canning of Bill Frieder was superb. Everyone knows the quote, 'The Michigan team will be coached by a Michigan man.' But Bo insisted that the quote everyone knows wasn't quite correct.

"'It was a bit simplified,' he said. 'What I actually said was, "We will have a man who works for Michigan coaching Michigan." I wasn't going to have the Arizona State basketball coach coaching Michigan. That was no big thing. Anyone would have done the same thing I did. Imagine being the athletics director and getting a call from a newspaper reporter at 11:00 at night telling you that your basketball coach had signed a contract with someone else.

"'He did not tell his players. He did not tell his coaches, and he did not tell me. Plus, the athletics director down there never called me to ask for permission to speak with Frieder. That whole thing was totally unethical.

"'He finally called the next day and said, "Bo, it's no problem. They have a jet waiting for me. I'll fly up and coach the team through the tournament." I said, "Like hell you will. You're finished here." I made Steve Fisher the coach that minute. I wasn't trying to win a national championship; I was just doing what was right, and I've gotten too much credit for it. It was a simple decision.'"

Alan Paul
sports journalist

"The first thing I knew about it, I got a call from Lynn Cook, who was Bo's secretary. It was 7:00 AM and she asked me to come in that morning at 7:30, the day before the tournament began. We were scheduled to practice and then leave for the first game.

"In his gruff, infamous way he said: 'Fisher, can you coach this team?' Then Bo simply told me that he wasn't going to let Bill coach the team and that I was going to be the interim head coach. Obviously, I was nervous. Not so much about coaching the team. Frieder was a master delegator and I knew what had to be done.

"It was more because of all the uncertainty. I knew I'd probably have to leave Michigan after seven years with the program with a new coach coming in. It would uproot my family. I might move to Arizona State with Bill after the tournament. There were also head coaching jobs coming open at my alma mater, Illinois State, and at Western Michigan, where I had been an assistant. All of that was on my mind before the first game.

"But when we started our tournament run I was pretty certain that I would get the job full-time; and Bo knew it, although he never said a word to me. He didn't have to say a word to me. That's just the way he was. I never even asked him why he chose me. There was an assistant who had been there longer than I had, but I was seen as Frieder's right-hand man.

"But what Bo did drew the team closer together. There was such a swirl of controversy that surrounded the team because of his decision that I think it created a single-minded purpose. It got everybody rallying around and believing the only people who thought we could win this thing was ourselves. If it hadn't been for spring football practice going on at the time, I really think he would have tried to coach the team himself.

"I asked him if he wanted to speak to the team before the final game against Seton Hall in Seattle. He said, 'If I went in and gave 'em a pep talk they'd all foul out by halftime.'

"We also had a very talented, good team, and you have to say that, too. In the NCAA Tournament, if you catch fire great things can happen. Bo couldn't have foreseen all that, of course, but the choice he made lit that fire."

Steve Fisher
Michigan basketball coach, 1989–97

Bo always felt that the Michigan basketball program needed to acquire the same aura as football to sustain its success. It bothered him that it never did.

"I've had former basketball players ask me why they can't build something like we have," he said. "A lot of it has to do with the coaches. I don't know that they have the same respect for their program.

"Can you imagine a head football coach at Michigan going off to take the job at Iowa State [like Johnny Orr] or Arizona State? Hell, no, he isn't going to go because he knows damn well he's got the best job in the United States. That's the difference."

"Bo's approach definitely had an impact on that team. I could see it. He was conveying an approach and an attitude they had never heard before. 'You're dealing with Bo, not Captain Go Easy on People.'

"It didn't make any difference what the sport is. You think I couldn't get a football team to play hard?"

Bobby Knight
former Indiana basketball coach, 1971–2000

"He got on each and every one of us when he met with the team. To me that was the turning point of the tournament."

Glen Rice
MVP of the 1989 NCAA Tournament

"I did not desert that team. I wanted to coach that team in the NCAA but the football coach wouldn't let me. I didn't go to the finals because I didn't want one man to keep me out of the dressing room."

Bill Frieder
former Michigan basketball coach, 1981–89

A conflict that isn't as well remembered as the others came in 1986, when Bo suspected that two players with eligibility remaining had signed with a pair of disreputable agents.

"I called them in to discuss the agent thing at least half a dozen times," he said. "I asked them point-blank each time if they had taken on an agent and every time they told me no.

"Right after the 1987 Rose Bowl, the FBI came to my office looking for the two guys, Bob Perryman and Garland Rivers. Perryman was already gone, but before he left he assured me once more that he hadn't signed with an agent until the season was over.

"Rivers was called in and he was interrogated right in my office. He admitted that he had signed before the 1986 season. I just couldn't believe it. Not that they had signed with the agents but that they could lie so often to my face, that they could betray me like that. That one really hurt.

"After the agents left I told Rivers, 'Son, you sold us down the river. You lied to me and you lied to this program. You risked the integrity of all the games we played this season.

There will be no more grant-in-aid for you. Clean out your locker. You are through here.' I never heard from either one of those players again."

Bo did testify at the trial of the two agents, however, in 1989 and had the satisfaction of seeing them convicted on federal racketeering charges.

CHAPTER
8

Practices

"I showed up for my first practice with my left arm in a sling. I'd dislocated it during an Ohio All-Star football game. Didn't make any difference. He still made me participate in spring drills. Star quarterbacks did not get special treatment in Bo's program.

"His practices were grueling. He'd make you repeat something, no matter how many times it took, until you got it right in his view. Everything ran on his whistle and he was involved in every aspect of practice."

Dennis Franklin
quarterback, 1974

"My freshman year there was a senior quarterback already in place with Mark Elzinga. In addition to that, no freshman had ever started a game at quarterback for Michigan. But it was a challenge and I decided I'd give it everything I had in practice and see what happened.

"I was a drop-back passer in high school and had never run an option before. But I was able to pick things up in a hurry and Bo never missed a thing on the practice field. He

Lloyd Carr still uses the same pregame meal of clam chowder, salad, steak, lasagna, and baked potato that Bo instituted during his coaching days.

was telling people that he'd never had a player who just had to be told once and he gets it. I didn't know any of this and he didn't even tell me that he'd made up his mind to start me in the opener at Wisconsin.

"I suspected something was up because I'd been working with the first team all week in practice. He said he didn't want to make me nervous. We won that one, but then we tied Stanford and Bo decided to start Elzinga against

Baylor the next week so I could clear my head. It was the only game I didn't start in four years.

"I think the play that really won him over was against Michigan State, which was always an underlined game on our schedule. It was at East Lansing, which is always tough, and it was 6–6 in the fourth quarter. We had a fourth-and-one at their 30. Had to go for it. And Bo called the option, which meant it came down to my decision.

"I kept it and was stopped short by their end, but I kept driving and got two yards on the play. Two plays later we scored and won the game, 16–6. Their coach, Denny Stolz, said it was the fourth-down play that won it. I don't think Bo ever had second thoughts about me after that."

Rick Leach
quarterback, 1978

"I was the 'Rudy' of Michigan football, the guy who managed to get on the field for one play during the Rose Bowl. And it was all because Bo never missed a thing in practice.

"In the practice before the 1980 game with Washington I was on the demo team during a punt drill, lining up on the defensive side. I managed to come off the corner and blocked the kick. Then I did it again.

"The Southern Cal coach, John Robinson, was watching our practice. He was a good friend of Bo's and Bo didn't like his first team getting shown up like that. He was yelling at his first team for letting me get in like that. He was so mad he walked over to me and started hitting me on the helmet with the yardstick he always carried in practice.

"But it got me into that game on that unit. I didn't block a kick, but we won it and I felt that I was a part of it. Then he put me on special teams all next season and that's where I won my letter. I was supposed to be a place-kicker but that didn't matter. I was playing for Michigan.

"I was the scout team punter, though. Once I was standing next to Bo at practice. He said, in his cordial way, 'How you doin', Tech? You're expendable.'

"Just a few seconds later the regular punter went down on a play. 'Coach, I guess I'm not expendable anymore,' I said. He just turned and hit me with the yardstick."

Karl Tech
special teams, 1981

"He was constantly talking in practice, always on you to make sure you were doing what you were supposed to be doing. No nonsense. It was a teaching session: respect, dedication, discipline. Being a champion on or off the field, and it didn't make any difference whether you were an All-American or on the demo team.

"But he had a light side. The last play at Friday practice was always a trick play, like a fake field goal. He'd let us have fun with it and everyone would end up laughing."

Mike Lantry
place-kicker, 1974

"We always stressed special teams in practice and I was the long snapper on kicks. We scored first on Notre Dame in the 1981 game. There was a tradition back then that after the first Michigan touchdown in the north end zone, students would throw down rolls of toilet paper on the field.

"There was a hand signal between me and the holder, B.J. Dickey, for when he was ready for the snap. But B.J. was disconcerted by all the paper raining down in the end zone and waved his hand for the officials to clear some of it away. That was our signal, and I snapped the ball.

"It hit him right on the side of the helmet. We had no chance to make the extra point. Our games with Notre Dame were always tight. The last two had been decided by two points, so every score was vital. Both B.J. and I were scared to death to go back to the sideline after that, but Bo didn't say a word.

"It helped that we won the game, 25–7. But it didn't help us at practice next week that the play was being shown on every late-night show in the country."

Larry Sweeney
center, 1983

"He had strong ideas about everything. Bo even drew up the menu for the Friday night meal before a home game when the entire team was at the hotel.

"It never varied. Bowl of clam chowder. Salad. Filet steak with sides of lasagna and baked potato. Ice-cream sundae. Then at lights out, there would be a knock at the door and room service would deliver hot chocolate and a cookie.

"That's how we do it to this day."

Lloyd Carr
Michigan head coach, 1995–present

"The organization was incredible. That's the only way Bo knew to do it. Every minute of the day, in season or off season, was mapped out for us.

"It was so funny to me early on. But I could see that the adjustments and wrinkles he would put in depending on the opponent were always effective. He knew exactly how to exploit their weaknesses, every game.

"We'd be out there and you'd see in their eyes they had no idea what we were doing, or what we were going to

Gary Moeller recalls that Bo would scrutinize every little detail of his team, their attitude, and sometimes even their surroundings during practice.

do next. It was like, Wow! Are we just so much smarter than anybody else? We were always better prepared than anyone we played."

Stan Edwards
running back, 1981

"He was aware of everything that went on during practice. He always said that the practice field helps you think young, how to think like a kid and feel the things they do. And if you think young, you'll stay young.

"He never missed a thing. During Ohio State week one year we were out on Ferry Field. Bo looked across to State Street and he saw a photographer taking pictures from the upper story of a house.

"He led all the coaches over there to confront the guy and called the police. He wanted to confiscate the film under the Trade Secrets Act. It turned out he was just a wire service photographer, but Bo was taking no chances.

"There was always a certain level of paranoia in this series. Some guys on the Ohio State staff once said that Woody insisted they only talk in whispers in the dressing room at Michigan Stadium because he was convinced it was bugged."

Gary Moeller
Michigan head coach, 1990–94

"Tuesday and Wednesday were the worst. Those practices could run for three hours easily. If he didn't like what he was seeing he'd blow that whistle and everything would have to start all over again, even if we were an hour and a half into it.

"He'd grab players from the pile by their facemask and just stare into their eyes 'to see if they were wusses,' he said. Bo didn't like wusses. He'd run around with his yardstick to measure the splits we were taking on the offensive line. It was intense, let me tell you.

"But the whole purpose was to remake you in the Michigan image. Bo didn't care what was popular or chic or flashy. He believed that nothing replaced hard work, and if you worked hard everything would come together when it mattered. Even during spring break, we were too scared to go off and have anything more than a beer. We knew he'd be testing us when we got back. I don't know if that kind of control is even possible today.

"We dreaded having him on the field with us. At least during the games he was off on the sideline and he could only yell at us. That's why if you beat one of his Michigan teams, you may get a win but it was gonna hurt."

Doug Daugherty
offensive lineman, 1989

"There was a motto all of us were familiar with: 'Blame no one. Expect nothing. Do something.' When you got the chance to stand out in practice, you'd better be ready to take it. Just to get on the travel squad was my goal as a freshman.

"The toughest practices we ever had were during that 1980 season. We lost two of our first three games, to Notre Dame and then to South Carolina. Well, Bo was not going to stand for it.

"Starting the next week, he matched the first-team offense against first-team defense in practice. That just wasn't done. But when we came through that I believe we were the toughest team in America. We didn't lose another game, they never scored a touchdown on us in the last five games of the season and we won Bo his first Rose Bowl.

"He always went against the biggest lineman in blocking drills to demonstrate the intensity he was looking for. When I was at Michigan, it was usually Ed Muransky, who was 6'7" and could have squashed Bo. He never did, though.

"He also had this delightful thing he called the Four Quarters test. It was to make sure you stayed in condition all year round. The first practice, you ran multiple 40-yard dashes, rested for one minute, then did it again. He repeated the cycle four times.

"The goal was to have all your times within half a second of each other. He was looking for consistency, not speed. If you passed, you were excused from running in the morning, which we all hated.

"Bo wanted to make us practice outdoors because he felt it toughened us up to be out there in bad weather conditions. Once in a while, though, he'd bring us into the indoor facility. I got hit under the facemask one time and started bleeding from a cut on my nose.

"Bo came rushing over and I said to myself, 'All right, I showed him some intensity.' Instead he started yelling at the assistants, 'Get him out of here, he's bleeding all over my new carpet.'"

Paul Girgash
linebacker, 1982

"We went 6–6 during the 1984 season. We'd just had one major injury after another, starting with our quarterback, Jim Harbaugh, in the fifth game. That did not count as an excuse with Bo.

"The spring practices before the next season were the worst. He cracked down on everything. We were practicing in full gear every day.

"But Bo knew we had to vanquish this weakness, this perception that Michigan wasn't tough enough to win anymore. He knew how easily that kind of mentality can take hold and he was going to drive it out before it could ever take root.

"I always think of 1985 as my best year as a player. We went 10–1–1, lost to Iowa with two seconds to play, and then beat a real good Nebraska team in the Fiesta Bowl. We finished ranked number two in the country and nobody was questioning our toughness anymore."

Jamie Morris
running back, 1987

"It rained for days before the 1972 Rose Bowl and there were no practice facilities available. Every football field in Los Angeles was soaked.

"Bo and Don Canham got in a car and drove everywhere, looking for a field. Finally, they heard a report that the field at Bakersfield Junior College, about 100 miles north, was dry. They put everyone on buses to go up there and get some practices in.

"I could see how annoyed he was when a local film crew found he was there and a camera crew stepped on the field during the practice. Bo practically ran up to the poor guys, yelling that no one goes on his field during practice. Afterward, he gave them a very nice interview, but he didn't like change when it concerned his practices. He felt afterward that the disruption in his schedule was a big reason why the team wasn't sharp and lost to Stanford in the game."

Bill Halls
former Michigan beat reporter,
Detroit News

"He was as fair as he could be. Seniors had no protected status with Bo. If you did what he wanted in practice, you played. It was strictly by ability and that's what made those practices so great.

"He beat the crap out of us, but we knew there was a reward for it."

Rich Caldarazzo
offensive lineman, 1969

"He had no compassion on the practice field. He was as tough as nails. It was like going to boot camp and he was your drill sergeant. He made it clear that on that practice field he was not there to be your friend. He demanded respect and perfection. We all felt that damned yardstick slapping on our helmets when we screwed up and then a hollering like there was no tomorrow.

"After going through that, you don't want to ever mess up again. There were no shades of gray when it came to this. It was either black or white."

Keith Mitchell
tight end, 1985

"I had to keep a supply of yardsticks on hand for him. He still thought he was an offensive line coach and when he saw one of his linemen lining up with the wrong stance or the wrong split, he'd whap him with the yardstick. I'd say three broken yardsticks made up a good practice for Bo.

"His search for perfection knew no bounds. The first practice after we had a 14–14 tie with Baylor, he came in and he was in a real bad mood. He wanted to know why one of our players, Mike Kenn, had a jersey with a bad number.

"A bad number in this case was one that crinkled instead of being smooth. 'I didn't think you'd notice,' I said. 'I notice everything,' he said. 'Now if you want to manage the goddamn equipment get busy and manage the goddamn equipment."

Jon Falk
Michigan equipment manager

"It was the fifth practice scrimmage of my freshman year and I was lined up at fullback, blocking for Jamie Morris. I'd played there and at linebacker in high school outside of Chicago, but Bo wanted me as a blocking back.

"They called a play and my assignment was to block the linebacker. It wasn't a great block, more like a stalemate. But it got the job done. The whistle blows, I turn around, and there's Jamie lying flat on his back. I'd gone the wrong way and blocked the wrong guy.

"Bo is furious. He comes running up and says, 'Who's my fullback?' There were a lot more expletives in it than that, actually. He turns to his running backs coach, Terrell

Burton, and says, 'What are you doing putting a freshman in there? You'll get my All-American killed!'

"Then he turns to me and says, 'Anderson, get out and stay out until you know the plays. I'm not going to waste time with freshmen.'

"A few plays later, they let me back in the scrimmage. It's an off-tackle play and I'm supposed to kick out on the end. I'm good and mad this time and I just blew him right off the play. The whistle blows and I'm feeling good, then I turn around and they're helping Jamie off his rear. I'd gone the wrong way again.

"This time Bo doesn't even bother with Burton. He starts right in on me. 'Anderson, start running,' he yells. 'Take a lap, get on State Street, head south until you get to Interstate 94, turn toward Chicago, and don't stop until you get home. You are the worst player we have ever recruited. I don't know why we are wasting money on you.'

"But there was a method to his madness. He got the best out of you. I went on to lead the team in tackles four straight years and won the Butkus Award as a senior. But only after they realized they had to shift me to linebacker."

Erick Anderson
linebacker, 1991

"It all worked because he knew how to get us laughing by saying something unexpected and out of character that we'd almost fall down. He'd say, 'The next man who makes a great play gets a milk shake,' and it just broke us up."

Dan Dierdorf
offensive lineman, 1970

"After losing to Missouri in Bo's first year, he was convinced the game had turned around because of a blocked punt. So in Tuesday practice we spent almost the whole time on punt drills.

"Bo yells out to the freshman team, 'I'll give you 20 dollars if you can block a punt.' Sure enough, they do and Bo takes off down the field in a fury.

"About half of the way to the punting team, he runs into Jim Brandstatter, an offensive lineman who was just jogging down the field. He starts swinging his arms at Jim like he was Bobby Knight going after a player. He figured Brandstatter had let in the punt blocker.

"Jerry Hanlon starts yelling at him, 'Bo, it wasn't him.' Bo just looked at Brandstatter and said, 'Well, you needed that anyway because you're a fat ass.'

"The warm fuzzy feelings came after graduation. When you played for Bo he was the coach, you were the player, end of story. You appreciated him a lot more afterward."

Reggie McKenzie
offensive lineman, 1971

"There was a Labor Day ritual. The team assembled for practice and Bo would say, 'Men, today is Labor Day and we are going to celebrate. By laboring.' There were no holidays for Bo during football season.

"But he was also fun-loving. Yes, the man who paces the sidelines and screams and yells and throws his headset is fun-loving. He would stage his own little bit of entertainment at the end of each practice week.

"He would line up at quarterback and throw one pass. One week, he got bored with that, though, and lined up as a tailback. But that didn't satisfy him, either. He decided to go in motion and then ran a down-and-out pattern in the end zone.

"Quarterback Michael Brown lofted the ball to him. It was falling short, but you know how competitive Bo is. He dove and did a double somersault, his hat flying off his head. Then he just lay on the ground motionless.

"Everyone froze. There was utter silence. This 59-year-old man had undergone two heart surgeries and he had just used his acrobatic skills to try and catch a pass that meant nothing.

"Then he jumped to his feet and started to laugh. It just cracked up everyone."

Michigan Daily
story on Bo's retirement, 1989

"During the summer of 1974, I had to take an extra class to keep up my eligibility. After one of our first team meetings before preseason practice, Bo called me into his office and told me the credit for that class hadn't arrived yet.

"I knew that I'd made an A in the four-hour course, but the professor had left on vacation a few weeks early without turning in my grade. I was bummed out, but he had assured me about the mark and it was all just a mix-up.

"Bo was not impressed. He had a special assignment for me until the professor returned. 'Strinko,' he said, 'you're going to have to run 10 100-yard dashes after the morning and afternoon practices for the entire preseason. And you'll have to beat me on every one of them.'

"Unless you've been through one of Bo's practices it's hard to explain how exhausted you were when they finished. So on the first day I line up at the end zone to start and Bo starts off on the 10-yard line. That doesn't seem like much of an advantage, but I was tired and not really in tip-top shape.

"Then just before we start he says, 'And for every one of these that I win, you'll have to run 10 more.' I think he was being kind to me because I won every one of those 100-yard dashes. I didn't think it fair at the time, but it taught me a lot about myself and what I could endure. It taught me a lot about him, too."

Steve Strinko
linebacker, 1974

"One of his favorite sayings was, 'Gentlemen, if we have to fight in the North Atlantic we're going to practice in the North Atlantic.' He'd then proceed to take us out of the warmth of our indoor facility into that howling Michigan November wind.

"His final words before we left for every road game were, 'I'm bringing 65 fightin' sons of bitches to take that place over.'"

Tim Schulte
linebacker, 1986

"It wasn't just the players who felt his intensity. I was a student assistant in the athletic department my freshman year, and for a kid right out of high school he was an intimidating figure.

"The first time I met him was at the first team meeting. He goes up to the grease board to write up some team rules, opens the marker, starts to write, and it's red ink. He looks at the marker, puts the cap on, and throws it all the way across the room, whizzing past my head.

"'We will have no red markers,' he shouts. 'Blue markers. Only blue markers.' I never brought another red or green marker into that meeting room."

Tom Lewand
Detroit Lions executive vice president
and COO

"Bo's idea about his motivational talks was that the ultimate purpose was for them to lead you to motivate yourself. My senior year we were having a tough time moving against Texas A&M. They had us down 10–7 late in the fourth quarter and we weren't getting it done.

"I came back to the sideline, went up to Bo, and started yelling, 'Run everything through me. Just run it through me.' He kind of smiled and then he did exactly that. He told me later that's what he was looking for from his players. And we won the game 14–10."

Dan Dierdorf
offensive lineman, 1970

CHAPTER
9

Bo among Others

The decade in which Bo and Woody Hayes coached directly against each other, from 1969 to 1978, brought the old rivalry to new heights of intensity. Winning that game meant winning the Big Ten title every one of those years. But more than that, it was the collision of two driven perfectionists who admired and even loved each other. That's what brought the game its special power.

Their overall records were almost identical. For Woody it was 238–72–10 and for Bo 234–65–8. Woody at OSU went 205–61–10 and Bo at Michigan was 194–48–5.

There are those who swear that Bo retired with his 234 career wins because he refused to pass his mentor's total. Between them, they accumulated 26 first-place finishes in the conference and produced 95 All-Americans and 42 first-round picks in the NFL draft.

Their record against each other was 5–4–1 for Bo. Over the first six years, the point totals were Michigan 74, Ohio State 75. It was that intense.

Bo on Woody: "I may have escaped from Columbus when I got the head coaching job at Miami. But I had a wonderful experience there because I coached for Woody when Woody was really Woody. He was the most irascible guy that ever lived and the

In the decade that they coached against each other, Bo and Woody elevated the Michigan-Ohio State rivalry to legendary status.

worst guy in the world to work for. But I wouldn't change that experience for anything in the world.

"He wanted me to stay on. He said that I'd be the next coach at Ohio State and that he'd be retiring in, oh, maybe four or five years. But I knew Woody and I knew it was time to go. He stayed on for another 16 years.

"Those 10 years we coached against each other were great. If that was war, you can sign me up anytime."

Woody on Bo: "If Bo is not a winner then I never saw one, and I should know. He's the second best in the country, after that old man down in Alabama [Bear Bryant].

"He beat me the last three games we played. We fought and quarreled for years but always considered ourselves great friends. We respected one another so damn much. Now that doesn't mean I didn't get so mad at him that I wanted to kick him in the...uh...groin.

"Those stories about how we used to get so mad when he was on my staff that we'd throw chairs at each other are way overblown. We just argued to beat hell. We just got damn mad. Well, sometimes we threw chairs...but not at each other. We were just in the same room when the chairs were thrown."

Bo enjoyed talking about the 1950 game between Miami and Cincinnati. The former coach at Miami, Sid Gillman, had gone to Cincy. The two schools are each other's oldest rival, and Gillman had taken some top players with him. Woody disliked Gillman intensely and pointed to this game. The motto was: "Let's show them what he left behind."

Miami won 28–0, and in the newsletter that went to recruits Woody wrote: "Bo Schembechler, our offensive tackle, draped the snow-covered field with Cincinnati defenders."

In later years, Woody would add: "It would have been 35–0 if a certain overeager tackle hadn't been offside."

The Woody story that Bo was reluctant to talk about, though, came when he got out of the army. Woody had promised him back at Miami that he would always make sure he'd have a job.

So Bo went to Columbus and showed up at Woody's office and Woody drove him to the unemployment bureau. It was his way of saying that he needed more experience before he could join the staff at Ohio State. But it hurt him deeply, even many years later.

Nevertheless, when Woody got in trouble after striking a Clemson player on the sidelines in the 1978 Gator Bowl, Bo had a secret meeting with him at the home of a mutual friend, Doyt Perry, the coach at Bowling Green State.

They talked for hours and he pleaded with Woody to apologize, telling him that he could save his job if he did. Woody absolutely refused. Bo said he insisted, "In my heart I know I didn't hit that player. I was just trying to wrestle the ball out of his arms because he was taunting my kids." A few days later he was fired as the Ohio State coach.

According to Bo's first biographer, Joe Falls, Bo also didn't like to talk about his first marriage, which ended in divorce. She had been Woody's secretary.

When Falls brought up the subject, Bo's response was, "We will *not* be talking about that." Joe insisted that it was an important part of his life story and Bo relented.

"All right," said Joe. "What was her name?"

Bo just looked at him blankly.

"Her name?" he persisted.

"I'm thinking," said Bo. Finally he blurted out, "Horses. She was crazy about horses."

Bo's relationship with athletics director Don Canham could also be tempestuous. Canham spoke about it in a 1981 interview with *Sports Illustrated.*

"Bo is oblivious to life; or, at least, that part of it that doesn't involve football. He is a delightful guy with a heck of a sense of humor. He also has a heck of a temper. I guess a lot of people do think of him as kicking dirt and throwing his hat and screaming at officials.

"But I've found that when he gets mad, it's time to get mad. And while he has a short fuse he also has a short memory.

"Right after I hired Bo I told him, 'Schembechler, if we have any trouble, it's going to be your fault...and I'm going to win.' He came in recently and started ranting about something and I just stood up and said, 'Schembechler, this is all your fault.' Then I walked out of the office. When I got back he was gone and nothing else was ever said about the subject.

"The only time I really got upset with him was when we were on my boat on Lake Erie and Bo kept wanting to make sure we were on course. I kept telling him it's just a pleasure cruise. There wasn't any course."

"Bo has two categories of things in his life, what matters and what doesn't matter. What matters is football. What doesn't matter is everything else. He is so dedicated that he doesn't even realize how he is coming off to other people."

Bob Ufer
late Michigan play-by-play announcer

"It was really unfair when people said that Bo never got out from under Woody's influence when it came to offense. When he had to change, he changed.

"When Southern Cal stopped our running game cold in the 1977 Rose Bowl he revised the offense and let me pass. When we went down 24–0 to Washington in the next Rose Bowl, he just turned it loose. I had the best passing day in my career; we had cut it to 27–20 and were down on their 8-yard line with two minutes left.

"Other years we would have tried to run it in. But Bo trusted me with the pass. I can still see that ball bouncing through Stan Edwards's hands, off his helmet, right on his shoulder pads, and the Washington guy grabbing it. That was it, but it was because Bo finally had confidence in the passing game that got us that close. They said it would have been the biggest comeback in Rose Bowl history if we had pulled it off."

Rick Leach
quarterback, 1978

It always annoyed Bo when his offense was criticized as being too predictable. That was heard most often after one of the Rose Bowl defeats.

"Our offense was the most complicated in the country," he said. "I know people looked at us as being a pretty simple operation. That's just not so. We were highly innovative and Gary Moeller was responsible for most of that. While I was handling all the public relations and running around representing the university, he was going around learning new stuff and teaching it to me.

"I had no doubts about turning over the job to him. Anybody would tell you he was the best coach in the country who wasn't a head coach. A great teacher.

"When he was offered the job at Illinois I told him, 'Gary, it's a great school and it has a great opportunity to win. But I want you to know before you go there that there isn't a single Big 10 football player on that team. Not one guy I'd want playing for Michigan.'

"He went down there anyhow and he was one guy who would not bend the rules. He's not going into the junior colleges. He's going into the high schools and bringing players in properly. I told him, 'Get five solid years, written in concrete, because that's how long it's going to take you to win.'

"I knew he wasn't going to win and he'd be a doormat for three years. So what happened? He lost for three years and they fired him, even though he had a contract for five years. I was glad to have him back."

When Illinois next came into Michigan Stadium, Bo ran up a 70–21 score on them. Bo never denied that it was payback for the way Moeller was treated.

The battles between Bo and Woody weren't limited to the football field. They frequently reached the flashpoint when it came to recruiting, too.

Being Ohio born and raised, Bo was quite successful at grabbing major talent from the state right from under Woody's nose. Hayes was infuriated by this, and Bo even suspected that he was being tracked on his recruiting trips south of the border.

"I would go in to talk to an Ohio prospect," Bo once said, "and when I was about to leave I would tell the young man, 'Now listen. Tomorrow Coach Hayes will be here and he'll want to talk to you about Ohio State.' The prospect would tell me that Woody wasn't scheduled to see him. He'd say, 'Coach Hayes was here a week ago; he's not coming tomorrow.'

"I would say, 'Trust me, Coach Hayes will be here tomorrow.' Sure enough, Woody would come marching into this kid's high school the next day. It was like he had spies around or something."

"I grew up in Fremont, Ohio, and I was being recruited by a lot of top schools, even Notre Dame and Southern California. But it came down to Michigan or Ohio State. Bo was working very hard to get me, though, and I committed to Michigan. But that wasn't the end of it.

"Just before the signing date, Coach Hayes drove up to Fremont and said he wanted one more shot at me. He made me look him right in the face and tell him that I was going to the school up north. When I told him, he said, 'Why?' It took all my courage to look him in the eye and say that I was going there because it was a better fit for me.

"Woody was not happy. He growled at me, stood up, and left. He never shook my hand. He said, among other things, 'Okay, we'll get along fine without you.' He never spoke to me again.

"But the story got a little strange later in my career. After a good experience at Michigan, I was drafted by the Denver

Broncos. One of my teammates was Randy Gradishar, who had been a great player at OSU. He would come to me during the season and pass along these little notes from Woody.

"I was amazed. They were very pleasant and encouraging. He would tell me to keep up the good work and things like that. We still never spoke; he just sent the notes.

"Toward the end of my career, I'd had about six surgeries on my knees and shoulder and figured I was done. I'd had a real good year the previous season, but then the team was sold and the entire coaching staff was fired. Dan Reeves was brought in as coach. He didn't know me and I figured that was it for sure. I'm gone.

"I made the last cut, though, and at the team meeting before our first regular-season game, Reeves is late. Another coach has to run the meeting. Finally Reeves comes in near the end and asks me to see him in his office.

"I figured I'd been cut or traded and I was kind of put out after going through the whole preseason. So I took the offensive with Reeves. 'You could have told me this before I got taped and dressed and all this crap,' I said. He looks at me and says, 'What the hell are you talking about? You made the team. Tell me something, though. Didn't you play for Michigan?'

"I told him that I did and he said, 'Well, Coach Hayes has been on my ass for the last 40 minutes. He told me that I was nuts if I didn't play you regularly. I don't know what kind of relationship you have, but you couldn't ask for a bigger fan.' Woody had built me up to Reeves like the second coming of Christ.

"That was 10 years after the last time we'd spoken. He'd been following my career that whole time, even though I had gone over to the archenemy. I always thought it was an unbelievable gesture. I loved playing for Bo at Michigan but I thought the world of Woody."

Rob Lytle
running back, 1976

"Bo and I talked when I came into the Big Ten to coach at Indiana. I told him that I knew I could never outrecruit Woody Hayes. All I could do was try to outwork him.

"He just looked at me. 'You will never see the day,' he said, 'when anybody will outwork Woody Hayes."

Lee Corso
TV commentator and former coach

"I was a captain of the Ohio State football team under Woody. He knew me quite well. When I was an assistant at Michigan, I attended one of his coaching clinics and gave one of the OSU staffers $10 to get Woody's autograph on his new book.

"A week or so later I got a letter with the $10 bill folded inside and a note saying, 'Woody says he won't autograph a book for any damned coach at Michigan.'"

Gary Moeller
Michigan head coach, 1990–94

"When Woody came back to Ann Arbor the next time after the big upset in 1969, he threw a major tantrum at the end of the game. We won 10–7, but he wanted a penalty to be called on a game-ending interception. He tore up the yard markers and was flinging them all over the place.

"Bo said later, 'I thought he was coming over to congratulate me, but I couldn't understand why he was bringing the yard markers along with him.'

"The two of them seldom talked during the '10-Year War.' Then in 1981, he [Woody] came to one of our practices. Bo called the team around and introduced him as 'our nemesis.' I think Woody really enjoyed that. [In 1987] He drove over to Dayton to introduce Bo at a meeting and then stayed for the entire speech. He died the following day."

Jerry Hanlon
Michigan assistant coach, 1969–91

"Woody was famous for his hatred of Michigan. He referred to it, of course, as 'that team up north,' but during those 10 years against Bo it seemed to intensify and expand to cover the entire state. One night he was on a recruiting trip in Michigan and his assistant coach noticed that they were about to run out of gas.

"Woody was half asleep in the passenger seat and the coach told him that they had to stop and fill up. Woody refused and made the guy drive on. The weather was starting to get bad. He was really getting scared that they would be stuck in the middle of nowhere and once again told his boss that they'd better pull over.

"'No, goddammit! We will not pull over and fill up. And I'll tell you exactly why we won't. It's because I won't buy one goddamn drop of gas in the state of Michigan. We'll coast and push this goddamn car to the Ohio line before I give this state a nickel of my money.'

"They barely made it across the border and sputtered into the first gas station they found in Ohio.

"What happened after he lost his first game coaching against Michigan is part of university lore. It was a 7–0 loss and the next day Woody called his entire staff and team together for a meeting. The film projector was turned on and the Michigan game came on the screen.

"After 10 minutes, he got up, walked over to the projector, picked it up, and threw it across the room. 'I will not subject the people of Columbus to that kind of football,' he said."

**www.bucknets.com/
osu history/coachhayes.htm**

"When I was named head coach at Michigan I could honestly say there were two important lessons I had learned from both Bo and Woody: run the ball and play defense."

Gary Moeller
Michigan head coach, 1990–94

"Woody was famous for his motivational speeches and techniques. One year he brought me back to speak to the team before the Michigan game. He wanted me to tell them what it was like to play in that game.

"I start in with whatever it was I said and all of a sudden Woody just goes into a frenzy. 'Yeah, but I mean tell 'em how it really bleeping was.' *Bam!* He hits me right in the stomach. 'Tell 'em it's like war.' *Bam!* He hits me again.

"'You gotta kill those sonsabitches.' *Bam!* I'm getting the snot beat out of me. It's like he's hitting the heavy bag. BAM! 'Now you tell 'em, Jim.' And I'm thinking to myself, *'How did I get into this?'*

"But you know what? Every guy who was there told me later, 'That was a great speech you gave.'"

Jim Stillwagon
Ohio State lineman, 1970

"He was always so competitive with Woody. I remember driving Bo to the airport one time when I was a graduate assistant. He was going down to Columbus to see Woody when he wasn't doing too well.

"'Woody's wife loves me,' Bo said. 'She always said I was one of her three favorite people in the world. Cary Grant was number one. Thomas Jefferson is number two, and then me. Woody didn't even make the top three.'"

Doug James
offensive lineman, '84

"My dad was a huge fan of Woody's and Bo knew it. Ohio State sent up a special plane to bring Bo down to Woody's funeral and he insisted that Dad go with him. They spent the day there and Bo even gave him a tour of Woody's office.

"He often said it was one of the most memorable days of his life."

Dave Rentschler
former M Club president, 1978–79

"After committing to Michigan, I went with Bo to a basketball game against Indiana. Bobby Knight went into a postgame rant, yelling at the media, cursing, seemingly out of control.

"After he left, Bo turned to me and said, 'What a coach!'"

Jamie Morris
running back, 1987

Bobby Knight called Bo "the best coach coaching anything in college sports."

"Several times Bo would be sick or ill and he would never miss a practice. Once he had kidney stones and I swear he passed the stones in the middle of practice just so he wouldn't miss it. But when Woody died, it was such an emotional roller coaster for him. We took two days off of spring drills to honor Woody."

David Key
defensive back, 1990

"He hired me sight unseen strictly on the recommendation of Bobby Knight. I was a graduate assistant at Indiana at the time and when I got the call I threw everything I owned in the back of my car and drove to Ann Arbor.

"There was no interview. We shook hands and I went to work. He was tremendously loyal and tough. When you get the chance to work for a man like that, you cherish it."

Cam Cameron
Miami Dolphins head coach

"Bo never forgot or forgave that 1979 Rose Bowl when we coached against each other. In the second quarter, Charles White dived into the end zone to score the second touchdown for USC. Unfortunately, the films showed that he didn't have the ball with him at the time. But the line judge ruled he had possession when he crossed the goal line. In those days before replays and appeals, there wasn't anything Bo could do.

"Charles always insisted he was 'just laying the ball down in the end zone like I always do for the refs to pick up.' Bo was absolutely furious about it, though, since we won the game, 17–10.

"In 1982, USC beat Notre Dame on a very similar call. Next time Bo saw me he said, 'You really perfected that play.'"

John Robinson
former USC head coach,
1976–82, 1993–97

"Bo was victimized twice by incompetent officials who blew calls in the Rose Bowl. Most people remember that phantom touchdown by White. That was nothing compared to what happened in the last game he ever coached, the 1990 Rose Bowl.

"The score was tied late in the fourth quarter and he called a fake punt. The Michigan kid ran for the first down, deep in Southern California territory, and this one official calls holding. Bo told me they went over those films over and over again and the kid they dropped the flag on wasn't even close to illegal contact.

"People remember Bo tripping on the phone wires running after the officials on that call. That's the picture that ran in all the newspapers. But they forget the terrible call that caused it. He ended up getting a 15-yard unsportsmanlike conduct penalty, which just added to the injustice. Michigan had to punt and Southern Cal drives in for the winning touchdown. Just a terrible way to go out.

"He was the best coach coaching anything in college sports."

Bobby Knight
former Indiana basketball coach,
1971–2000

"I was the wrestling coach at Michigan from 1970 to 1974 and got to know Bo then. I applied for the job as athletics director at Oregon and he made a call out there for me.

"I tried to thank him for that but all he did was wave his hand and say, 'All I did was tell them you weren't a jerk.'"

Rick Bay
former Ohio State athletics director,
1984–87

"Everyone remembers that it was Mike White who coached against Bear Bryant in his last game. I know for a fact that White remembers. So when they look at the records, they'll see it was me coaching against Bo.

"It was still a shock to realize it, though. I always thought he'd coach until he was 80."

Larry Smith
coach at Southern California in the 1990
Rose Bowl and a former Michigan assistant

"Bo coached the line at Northwestern for me and we didn't win a game all year. We'd sit there until 1:00, 2:00 in the morning trying to figure out what was wrong. Finally, Bo came to me and told me that he had it figured out. Our seniors were all playing for themselves and not the team.

"He told me later that he learned more in that zero-win season than he ever had in his life. He learned that you had to rely on your seniors to set the tone for the team and you had to instill the attitude of playing for the team into them when they're freshmen and sophomores. Because if the seniors are dogging it, you know you're in trouble.

"When everything is going well and you're winning, that's one thing. But when you're losing week after week, you find some things out about the game and the people you've got playing it.

"More than that, though, Bo had the ability to dissect every movement involved in blocking techniques and teach it to others. He could take all those physical movements apart and put them back together again."

Ara Parseghian
former Notre Dame coach, 1964–74

"I remember a statement he made a few years after he stopped coaching. I thought it was very significant. He was speaking to one of our coaches conventions and he already was kind of giving the old-timers' view.

"I'll never forget that he said he wished he'd never stopped coaching. He said that if he'd gone on he'd probably be dead by now. Here I was, this 60-something-year-old man, listening to him and thinking that coaching meant so much to him that he wished he'd gone on even if it shortened his life.

"And I thought, *Now that's commitment.*"

Bobby Bowden
Florida State head coach, 1976-present

"He called me into his office when I got the head coaching job and he told me, 'There are going to be days when you have doubts and ask yourself whether you're good enough, when you doubt your ability. I know because I've had them myself.

Bobby Bowden was moved by Bo's commitment to coaching when Bo mused that he might have retired too early.

"'When you have them, get rid of them. Because you're good enough.'

"He absolutely refused to allow me to accept a job offer from Lou Holtz at Notre Dame. 'No,' he said. 'You're Michigan.' And that settled that.

"I can honestly say that I've never gone on the field at Michigan with anything other than the expectation of winning the game. Fritz Crisler used to say that you can't buy a tradition like that. That's what I saw in Bo—the belief and commitment to win."

Lloyd Carr
Michigan head coach, 1995–present

"I was scouting for Washington and happened to pass by Bo's office when he and Jerry Hanlon were screaming at each other. They were hollering, going back and forth. I turned around and thought to myself, 'Well, this isn't a real good time. I better come back another day.'

"Bo told me later it was just normal. That was just how they expressed themselves and they both understood it. It sure sounded like screaming to me, though."

Jim Mora
former Atlanta Falcons coach, 2004–06

Longtime assistant coach Bill McCartney, who would later found a Christian group for men called the Promise Keepers, was fond of quoting the Bible to explain Bo's outbursts of temper. "It's in Proverbs 28:23," he said. "'He who rebukes a man will in the end gain more favor than he who has a flattering tongue.'"

"Once in a while, he'd ask me to rent a video that we'd watch together. It had to be short. It couldn't be about football. It couldn't feature an actor he didn't like.

"One time we settled on the movie *Being There*, which seemed to fit all the requirements. Within five minutes he was fast asleep, woke up right at the end, and said, 'That is the worst movie I've ever seen.'"

Jon Falk
Michigan equipment manager

"To outsiders it may have sounded a little vociferous, but we knew how to handle each other. And I knew when to shut up. Well, sometimes I didn't.

"I was fired numerous times. I was run out of the building before practice and then had to come in and take over because no one else knew how to run the practice the way he wanted it. The secret of coaching for Bo was getting hired one more time than you were fired.

"He made me mad but all arguing stopped on the field...but not on the phones. When I was stationed in the press box and on the phone with him, you wouldn't want to hear a tape of the conversations we had. You'd have to bleep out most of it. But he created a situation where you wanted to go to work in the morning.

"The other big thing is that we went to work hoping we could keep up with the other guys on the staff. Bo surrounded himself with incredible talent. You never went in saying, 'Whose job am I going to have to do today?' Or 'Who'll cover for me?' To me, that's the sign of a great leader.

"Even after both of us had retired we kept arguing about what was going on in today's football. Even to the point of hollering. I know one thing. I have to go to heaven now just so we can continue our argument."

Jerry Hanlon
assistant coach, 1969–91

One of the stories Bo delighted in telling is when he was named an assistant to Bear Bryant in a postseason All-Star game. Bear put him in charge of the offense and told him to put in a gadget play of some kind for his All-American running back, Johnny Musso.

As it turned out, Bear was more than willing to turn over all the coaching duties to Bo and enjoy the week in the sun. By the fourth quarter of the game, their team was way ahead and Bryant suddenly realized that he hadn't seen the play for Musso yet.

He called Bo over and insisted that they run the play. They did and Musso broke off a long run. The coaches on the other team were furious at what they thought was Bo rubbing it in. They were screaming at him from across the field. All he could do was yell back at them, "It wasn't me. I'm not the coach. Bear's the coach."

"If he talked long enough he could convince you that an apple was an orange. You'd listen for a while and say, 'Sure enough. It's an orange.'"

Lou Holtz
TV analyst and former Notre Dame coach

"He met Elvis once. It's true. Bo was in Las Vegas and somehow after the show he ended up backstage with the King. Bo didn't really know what to say so he paid the singer a compliment on his jumpsuits.

"The next thing he knew, he was back in a private closet with Elvis showing him his collection of rhinestone-covered costumes. He told Bo how much they cost and that he never wore them more than once and then they were shipped to some museum.

"There was, Bo recalled, an awkward pause, just the two of them, alone with those jumpsuits, and then they came back and joined the crowd. Years later, I asked Bo what he thought of that encounter.

"'I thought that I don't want to be him,' he said."

Mitch Albom
author of *Bo*

CHAPTER
10

Boys to Men

Bo announced his intention to step down as coach almost absent-mindedly to a sociology class he was speaking to on campus. "I won't get the chance to sit in that new building [Schembechler Hall] they're putting up," he said.

Almost immediately, phone lines lit up across Ann Arbor and in newsrooms all across the state of Michigan. Bo finally had to announce it to his team, two weeks before they were scheduled to leave for Pasadena and the 1990 Rose Bowl.

Bo said that he'd been thinking about his decision for weeks. "The time it really washed over me was at the end of the Ohio State game," he said. "I looked up and told myself, *This is the last time in Michigan Stadium and I'll never be involved in one of these games again.* It was almost too much for me.

"But I really made up my mind earlier in that year, and it had very little to do with my physical health. We were running a practice and I was aware that one of our linebackers, J.J. Grant, was nursing an injury. I don't know what happened; my attention was diverted or something and the next thing I knew J.J. had reinjured himself.

"I was losing my concentration. I knew that sometimes I couldn't remember a guy's name that I had coached and I had to take out an old team photograph and look at it. That bothered

When Bo announced he was stepping down as coach, he and the Michigan family cried together before Bo gave a final bow.

me, but this was completely different. That was the start of it, when I knew it was time to get out.

"My greatest achievement is that I coached a lot of great guys and they are my friends today. That means more to me than anything else. Everyone talks about bowl games and records and how many games you won, but your association with the players is more important than anything else. I never gave a damn about what anyone else ever said about me as long as I got along with my players.

"They were the only ones I had to prove myself to and I had to do that every day. I wasn't going to get fired. I wasn't going to lose a lot of games. I was hard on my players. I was terrible. But when it was all over, when the last practice was held and the last game was played, they understood what I was trying to do and they became my friends. Not all of them, but most of them.

"I was smart enough to know you have to learn how to control your temper. It's just when things weren't right, I reacted aggressively. They embellish the hell out of the stories, too. To hear them talk I was the toughest, meanest bastard who ever lived. I know that wasn't true.

"But there was no hanky-panky. We went by the book and we played as hard and as tough as we could.

"I loved coaching college football. Because you have to make do with what you've got. I may want a better player, but I can't trade for one or pick up a free agent, so I'll coach the hell out of the guy because he has to play—and because he's mine."

"He started saying something about the thing that he would miss most was the association he had with his players, the guys who went to war for him, and he couldn't continue. We could see that he was crying and so were most of us. It was so damn strange; not only the announcement that he wasn't going to be the coach anymore but to see him cry. We just didn't think he'd ever show that kind of emotion."

Derrick Walker
tight end and team captain, 1989

"Looking back on it, I could tell he was slowing down. He was just not as hyper, not as active on the practice field as he'd been when I was a freshman. Then he was running all over the place, talking to everyone. He was the most powerful presence I'd ever known.

"Bo wouldn't let us get it into our heads that we were supposed to win the last game for him. We were to win it for the seniors. That was always the way he was."

Allen Jefferson
running back, 1990

"I told him he didn't have to quit. I'll do the work. All you have to do is stand on the sidelines and cross your arms if you want. There are other coaches who actually have done that. He just shook his head and said, 'That's not me.'"

Gary Moeller
Bo's successor as Michigan head coach,
1990–94

"The biggest thing I learned about management from Bo is that anyone who wanted an appointment with him could get it. That's how it was at Michigan. All I had to do was walk in his office. When I became president and CEO of Steelcase Furniture, I made it clear that all anyone had to do to see me is pick up the phone. I'll work them into my schedule.

"The thing is that's the best way to find out what is really going on in the plant. You learn about the things that get by your subordinates or that they might not want you to know."

Jim Hackett
center, 1976

"During the middle of the season he took the time to write me a letter of recommendation for a job at Comerica Bank. Now I'm the vice president of a loan group there, but even after 25 years he'd remember where I worked and always asked how come I wasn't president of Comerica yet. It amazed me.

"There were times when Bo didn't seem to realize who he was, the stature he had. I'd be on a bus with him as we were going to a speech at a fund-raiser, and he was nervous. 'I have to go out and ask the bigwigs for money,' he'd say.

"It never seemed to occur to him that these guys would be hanging on every word he had to say."

Karl Tech
special teams, 1981

"I'd injured my knee as a freshman quarterback and it took a long time to get better. There was no redshirt rule in the Big Ten then so I pretty much lost a year of eligibility and when I came back I was down on the depth chart.

"Bo didn't give up on me, though, and he asked me if I wanted to try playing safety on defense. I jumped at the chance and started all 10 games there in my senior season. I was drafted by the New York Jets, but before I got to their camp I hurt my eye in a freak accident. It affected my balance, I couldn't run, and I really had no chance to make the team.

"Bo went to some Michigan alumni in my hometown, Cleveland, and got some money together so I could finish work on my degree. Then he brought me back as an assistant coach with the freshman team to work with Dennis Franklin. He didn't have to do any of this. I sure wasn't one of his stars. But he did it."

Jim Betts
safety, 1970

"I am a screenwriter for TV and movies and I've done several scripts that were sports related. *Mr. 3000. Like Mike.* But every time he saw me, Bo would ask, 'When are you going to write a good sports movie?'"

Keith Mitchell
tight end, 1980

"The high point of every season for me was the one-on-one meeting with Bo. He would talk about the past season, goals for next year, how your academics were going.

"Every guy on the team got that personal attention and for those of us who didn't play that much it was especially meaningful. After graduation, my talks with him were even more meaningful. He always knew who I was immediately. It was, 'Hey, Mike, how ya doin'?' every time, and believe me, I was not one of the more memorable guys he ever coached.

"He knew I was coaching high school football in Pennsylvania and he'd always ask about my team. If you were one of Bo's Boys he always seemed to know what was going on in your life. I keep a Bo bobble head on my desk and I also instill in my players what is meant by Bo Time: you show up five minutes early.

"We even sing 'The Victors' with a few word changes and I try to make sure there is a strong sense of tradition in our program. That comes from Bo.

"One of the happiest things in my life was that I got the chance to tell him what he meant to me and the impact he had on my life. I'm not just talking about football and how I use his philosophies with my team. I use the same sort of thing in my social studies classroom. I talk to my own children about it. It never was just about football. It was about life and how you carry yourself through the ups and downs.

"The effects will ripple on for successive generations."

Mike Melnyk
place-kicker, 1984

"Bottom line was that if you persevered and never gave up you would accomplish your goals. He knew I wanted to be a doctor and sometimes when things weren't going too well, I kept at it because I didn't want to let him down.

"In all honesty, the first year of playing for Bo was tougher than anything I encountered in medical school. That slogan about those who stay being champions applies to every experience in life, anything you want to achieve that is difficult."

Marc Milia
center, 1993

"After leaving school, I was drafted in the fifth round by the Atlanta Falcons. Then everything fell apart.

"Within a year, I lost my mom, a dear aunt, and an uncle and went down with a bad knee injury. I started to drink to get through it and I just kept getting in deeper and deeper, liquor and drugs. My wife divorced me, I lost custody of my three kids, then I was sentenced to 21 years for having knowledge of a bank robbery.

"I did hard time and when I was paroled I ended up homeless. I tell everyone who wants to hear my story that it was what I learned from Bo that finally gave me the courage to get back up on my feet. I heard the voice of the Lord telling me to come forth. It was August 17, 1997, and my new life began. But that voice sounded a lot like Bo.

"He had taught me how to be a man. It was integrity, hard work, and always, always to get back up when you get knocked down. He was not only my inspiration; he was a friend I could talk to when things were at their worst. He was part of my family.

"I went back to school at the University of Nevada–Las Vegas and in 2003 I earned my Ph.D. I now work with the Salvation Army in Detroit and the name I gave my group was Get Back Up, Inc."

Billy Taylor
running back, 1971

"When he joined the Detroit Tigers he arranged for one his former players, Mike Gillette, to have a tryout as a catcher. He had been a place-kicker in college, but Bo insisted this was not being done as a favor. 'I know an athlete when I see one,' he said. 'Athletes are athletes.'

"Gillette didn't get picked up by the organization, but Bo was absolutely right. Finding athletes was his forte. He saw the little things that made a big difference.

"He also brought in techniques that we didn't have before. Video equipment for all our minor league teams, for example. If our goal was to cultivate the farm system and grow from within, it just didn't make sense to him that our minor leaguers couldn't see videos of their performance. Same thing with strength and conditioning drills. In many respects, baseball was lagging far behind college football, and Bo caught us up."

Joe McDonald
former Tigers executive, 1987–92

"I never understood the questions about Bo and baseball. The easiest thing in the world is to work with people who are successful. I know they know what I'm talking about when I'm talking.

"He also did one thing I didn't believe would be possible. When he was with the Tigers he changed me from rooting for Southern California to rooting for Michigan. I had been a big USC fan from the time I was a kid. I used to hang out at the campus so I could watch their baseball team practice. But I got to know that Bo stood for honesty and I switched to Michigan."

Sparky Anderson
former Tigers manager, 1979–95

Detroit Tigers manager Sparky Anderson and team president Bo Schembechler stroll through the infield at Fenway Park before opening the season in April 1990.

"He didn't have a prejudiced bone in his body, but he told us that he didn't want us participating in any campus demonstrations. This was 1969, remember, and there was a demonstration of some kind going on at Michigan practically every day.

"He said it would be bad for the team. But at the same time he was teaching us to be true to our convictions and not be afraid to speak out for what we believed. Only wait until you graduate. He didn't want to hear about it until then."

Rich Caldarazzo
offensive lineman, 1969

"Braylon [Edwards' son] had a unique advantage at Michigan because I'd been taking him to the practice facilities since he was five years old. The two of them would close the door to Bo's office and talk about all different things.

"He inspired Braylon tremendously, and while he never played for him, Bo was a big part of his success. It's a major reason he stayed all four years to get his degree.

"When I was playing, the guys who left school early to turn pro, Bo would urge them to come back and get the diploma. I know for a fact that he even paid the way of some of them to do it. Think of it. They were making good money in the pros and he was writing the checks for them. That's the kind of person he was."

Stan Edwards
running back, 1981

"Bo gave me my MBA referrals, and when I needed any kind of referral for a job he would always come through. I don't think there was a day that went by he didn't get 10 to 15 calls from former players, and a good many of them needed a favor. He never hesitated.

"I returned to the program with the understanding that I would stay four years to build up my résumé, decide what kind of business I wanted to start, and Bo would assist me. I stayed for 21 years and he made me assistant athletics director.

"I am now a lead management consultant and all I do essentially is build on the principles he taught us. Discipline. Understanding who you are. Identifying your values and never compromising them. That's what marks you as an individual and separates you from the crowd.

"You must have a vision of excellence that goes beyond what anyone can imagine, and that's what you strive for every day. It's all embodied in that saying of Bo's: 'You get better or you get worse every day. You never stay the same.'"

Fritz Seyferth
running back, 1971

"He even felt a responsibility for things like the polls. 'When I was coaching,' he'd say, 'I couldn't be completely fair to the teams I didn't see. I would usually pass it on to a member of my staff. I just didn't have the time.

"'Now not only do I have the time but I can look at 20 game tapes every week. I know more about college teams throughout the country than I ever did when I was coaching.'"

Lloyd Carr
Michigan head coach, 1995–present

"Bo never intended for the building to be called Schembechler Hall. Its official name was supposed to be the Center of Champions. But people call a building by the name they feel is appropriate.

"It attracted some criticism at first. But that's what a good design should do. I was pleased about the controversy. It was not meant to be pushed in the background. The intent was to express what it was about, and if people see in that a reflection of Bo, that's fine.

"Some see a football helmet there. Some see the trajectory of a football. I call it a touchdown pass."

Gunnar Birkerts
architect of Schembechler Hall,
for which Bo raised most of the
$12 million construction cost

"When some people summed up his career they pointed out that he had never won a national championship. Was he obsessed by it? Well, he was only human and I'm sure that sitting alone in his office there were times when he thought about the times he had come close and never did it.

"But anyone who knew Bo knew he was not an unfulfilled man. He was a pretty satisfied guy. To criticize him for not winning a national title is lunacy."

Dan Dierdorf
offensive lineman, 1970

Former Nebraska coach Tom Osborne could relate to the lifelong quest for excellence that Bo sought at Michigan.

"I know how he felt and we even discussed it once or twice. It wasn't until the end of my career that I accomplished it, and I was hearing the same things he was.

"It's like Captain Ahab chasing the white whale. The focus always shifts to that, the one thing you haven't done. And I heard it more within my own state than I ever did nationally. It was frustrating."

Tom Osborne
former Nebraska coach, 1973–97

"That thing about Bo not being able to win the big one is ridiculous, a bum rap. Most coaches never even get in the position to play in the big one. Just getting there is a tremendous achievement."

Ara Parseghian
former Notre Dame coach, 1964–74

CHAPTER
11

Fourth Down

"After we beat Ohio State in 1985 he called me into his office and said, 'Do you realize how much you meant to Michigan today?' I treasure that moment to this very day."

Jim Harbaugh
quarterback, 1986

"It was tremendous that he stayed on campus after his retirement. It gave every player who came in a chance to touch and listen to the man who symbolized what makes Michigan football great."

Reggie McKenzie
offensive lineman, 1971

"I sometimes suggested that, perhaps, he could temper his passions toward the officials. It wasn't good for his health and it also might get him suspended.

"He said, 'I'll try.' And he did. But he never lost that passion. As president of the university I did take pride in

Bo's unrelenting focus on football sometimes strained not only his family life, but his health.

the fact that he never tolerated any hanky-panky and never stood for any nonsense from any of his athletes."

Robben Fleming
University of Michigan president,
1968–79, 1988

"I cleaned out his locker as soon as he announced his retirement. He came down to the locker room and confronted me. He said, 'That was pretty damn quick, Falk.'

"I just hit him with the line from *The Natural:* 'They come and they go, Hobbs. They come and they go.'"

Jon Falk
football equipment manager

"There were some questions when I hired him as president of the Detroit Tigers. After all, his reason for giving up the coaching job was health.

"But he said, 'Stress never bothered me. I have to have a challenge. I'm not going to take it easy no matter what happens.'

"The fact is Bo didn't know how not to work. You couldn't hold him back. We were looking for a successor to Jim Campbell, who was getting ready to step down. He and Jim were pretty close and Jim once asked him, 'What will you do when you finish coaching?' Bo answered, 'I want your job.'

"Jim called me the next day and said, 'Our search is over.'"

Tom Monaghan
Detroit Tigers former owner, 1983–92

Unfortunately, Bo's relationship with Monaghan ended poorly, leading to what Bo later called "the toughest time of my life." A little more than two years after leaving Michigan to join the Tigers, both he and Campbell were fired in advance of Monaghan selling the team to his fellow pizza baron, Mike Ilitch.

"We had been trying to rebuild the farm system and get a new stadium approved and he [Monaghan] was pulling money out of the franchise," Bo said. "We didn't have the money to compete. That last season [1992] was pure misery. Then two weeks after I was canned, Millie died of cancer."

They had married in 1968, fixed up by friends. She was a single mom, trying to raise three kids, working as a nurse in St. Louis. At their first scheduled meeting in Oxford, Ohio, Bo got sidetracked with something else and never showed up. Eventually, they did have their meeting—it wasn't really a date—and she saw immediately that Bo had won over her three sons as soon as he walked through the front door. Within four months they were married.

Millie's joke was that Bo had made a list of things to accomplish during the year. It read: (1) Finish recruiting. (2) Finish spring practice. (3) Find wife. (4) Get married. (5) Start fall drills.

Their marriage was not perfect and Millie often suffered in silence when her husband was off on recruiting trips or making speeches or getting swept up in the madness of the football season. But now that she was gone, Bo sank into a depression unlike anything he had ever known. With his breach-of-contract suit with Monaghan going on at the same time, it was more than he could handle.

"Finally, I woke up one day, looked in the mirror, and said, 'Enough of this. This isn't me and it stops today.'"

But he still had his moments when football was on his mind. "I sometimes thought that I let the doctors scare me a little and nothing could have been as bad at Michigan as that mess I walked into with the Tigers," he said. "We'd been to two straight Rose Bowls and the 1990 and 1991 teams were filled with guys I'd recruited. I would have had a pat hand."

A few months later, he met Cathy Aikens in Florida. She had no idea who he was and asked in all seriousness if coaching football "was all you did." They were married in 1993 and he finally began to enjoy his retirement.

"He came down to my hospital to talk about cardiac health. He told the patients that for his entire career at Michigan—one of the most stressful jobs in the country—he had a bad heart.

"It was the first time I'd ever heard him discuss it. That's when I truly grasped the courage and strength it took for him to continue in a job that had given him his medical problem.

"I played for him 20 years after his first heart attack. He'd had two open-heart surgeries by then and went through two or three cardiac arrests. That day at the hospital was the last time I saw him and the first time I really understood what he was made of."

Marc Milia
center, 1993

"He enjoyed coming to Lions practices, and when he was here many people knew he was having circulatory problems with his legs. One year I said, 'Hey Coach, I'll get you a cart.'

"He looked over at me and said, 'I don't need no stinking cart. I'll walk.' To have had the health problems he did for the last 36 years of his life and still go on working so hard for the University of Michigan... All you can say is that he got the most out of everything he took up."

Tom Lewand
Detroit Lions executive
vice president and COO

"After his first heart attack he took up swimming as an exercise and he'd come over to the Matt Mann Pool. Even at something like swimming he was always trying to improve because he could not accept the status quo.

"We gave him some tips on his stroke so that he could improve his workouts and he was always eager to learn."

Don Peterson
swimming, 1973

Bo and Don Canham enjoyed a long and successful relationship working together for the Wolverines.

Bo said later that he was fully aware during his first heart attack that something was wrong. As he walked up the hill to where the team was staying in Pasadena, he felt chest pains and a shooting pain down his arm.

"I was supposed to introduce [university president Robben] Fleming that night," he said. "I got through that and then sat down immediately. Don Canham leaned over to me and whispered that it was impolite to sit down and that I should have stayed at the podium to greet Fleming.

"What was I supposed to tell Canham, 'Pardon me, but I think I'm having a heart attack'?

"The thing that I remember most, though, was lying in that hospital bed with all kinds of tubes sticking out of me, and George Allen, who was coaching the Los Angeles Rams, came in to visit me. He looked at me and said: 'Bo. Bo. Tell me. What can I do to prevent this from happening to me?'

"I'd put on 25 pounds in that first year, just by nervous eating. I was out recruiting constantly. The week of the Ohio State game there was a sleet storm and I was out there shoveling with the maintenance crew to get the practice field ready. It was really stupid."

"I'll never forget that first heart attack, the night before the Rose Bowl in 1970. We knew something was up when he was late before we left for the game from the hotel, because Bo was never late. 'Bo Time' meant five minutes early.

"When they told us what had happened guys were crying on the bus. We walked out of the tunnel that day at the start of the game. We didn't run, and that was something I've never seen before or since at Michigan."

Rich Caldarazzo
offensive lineman, 1969

Offensive lineman Rich Caldarazzo recalls how stunned the team was after learning of Bo's heart attack the night before the 1970 Rose Bowl.

"After winning the 1989 Rose Bowl, he got on the bus and lit up a nine-inch cigar. 'Men, my damn doctors told me not to smoke cigars,' he said. 'I told them there were two occasions on which I would. Winning a national championship or winning the Rose Bowl.' He then started puffing away and we all cheered.

"Here's a piece of trivia. We went back there to play UCLA next season and became the only Michigan team ever to win twice at the Rose Bowl in the same calendar year."

Doug Daugherty
offensive lineman, 1989

"I became a fund-raiser for University Hospital, and as his heart grew progressively weaker we got him into the cardiovascular center there. That's what kept him alive for his last five years.

"He was so enthusiastic he became a member of our national advisory board and one of our most prolific fund-raisers. The staff loved him. They'd ask him how much he weighed and he'd say: 'I'm 205 pounds of twisted blue steel.'"

Fritz Seyferth
running back, 1971

"When I was a high school student they used to bring us in on game days for free so the stadium would look as if there were more people in it. When I sat on the University Board of Regents we had to vote on plans to reconfigure the stadium to get in more people.

"That's all Bo. That's what he accomplished."

Dave Brandon
end, 1973, and CEO of Domino's Pizza

"I hear people say that there could never be another Bo in college football the way the sport is today. I disagree.

"All that person would have to do is outwork every competitor. He'd have to appreciate the perfectly blocked off tackle play more than the perfectly thrown spiral. He'd have to never break a rule.

"He'd have to have a clear understanding of right and wrong and always choose right. He'd have to value loyalty to his school over making millions somewhere else. When his school offered him more money, he'd have to insist on sharing it with his assistant coaches.

"He'd have to relish preparation as much as the games. He'd have to believe the tougher, better prepared, more fundamentally sound team will win many more times than it will lose. He'd have to care for his coaches and players as if they were family, but demand they work harder than they ever had before and give more than they ever thought they were capable of giving.

"He'd have to build an enduring legacy of integrity, loyalty, and trust. He'd have to understand that there are no shortcuts to lasting success. He'd have to know humility and place the team above everything else.

"That's all."

Craig Dunaway
M Club president, 2006–07

"You can't begin to imagine the positive impact he had on so many lives. I don't just mean those who played for him, but the lessons they passed on to others that they learned from him. I think most of us would like to believe that during our lifetime we made a difference. Well, he did.

"But I think he had the wording of that sign a little wrong. It should have read, 'Those who stay will be blessed.'"

Dave Metz
offensive lineman, 1974

"I try to avoid going by his old office in Schembechler Hall. It's like you expect him still to be there and when he isn't you have that fleeting moment when you almost say to yourself, 'I wonder when he'll be back.' That's the toughest part."

Jamie Morris
running back, 1987

"I remember the last Michigan football reunion Bo attended. There must have been 500 of us there. He told us that after a round of golf he'd sit on the patio of his condo in Florida. He talked about his health, how bad he felt, the medication he had to take every day.

"His shoulder ached—and he had to remind us that he had been a pretty good left-handed pitcher at Miami University. He could hardly feel his feet because of diabetes, and in general he felt like crap.

"But, he said, he'd watch the sun set over the Gulf of Mexico, take a sip of beer, and say to himself, 'I'm the luckiest son of a bitch to have ever lived to have been the football coach at Michigan.'

"I still get chills when I think about that. I feel I was just as lucky to have known him."

Doug James
offensive lineman, 1984

"I was doing some running at Michigan Stadium when I got the news of his death. He was such a tough old man I thought they could just keep patching him up forever.

"I was the only one in the stadium and there was just utter silence in there. I kept thinking that he was the one who had filled this place every week, and how enormous it looks when there's no one there."

Mike Lantry
place-kicker, 1974

"I was a whistle-blower is all. I was one of the guys and I hung around a long time. I was a hard-nosed bastard but I was honest. I had some success and when I walked away I had the Michigan stamp on me."

Glenn "Bo" Schembechler
1929–2006

CHAPTER 12

My Favorite Bo Memories

They held the introductory press conference two days after Christmas, 1968, in the old Events Building on campus. We knew right away this was a very special event because there was hot coffee and pastries for the media. Michigan has a reputation for being a bit parsimonious on this score. Even today, the pressbox is noted for hot dogs and cider, while up at Michigan State you may be served lamb or turkey from the university farm. We journalists keep track of such things.

Bo walked in wearing a tie that was probably the closest he could come to maize and blue. It was more yellow than maize, though, and there was also a stripe of red in it. But he got marks for trying, especially since almost no one in the room had ever heard of him.

The one thing I clearly recall him saying was that he was always battling his weight because he didn't smoke, and that he ate too much after a game because of nervous energy, then went right to bed. That would come back underlined in red just one year and four days later, when he had his first heart attack on the eve of the Rose Bowl.

When someone asked him how late he slept on Sunday mornings, he said 10:00. The obvious follow-up question was why and Bo immediately responded: "Because that's when the game films are ready."

The other press conference that stands out in my mind was the one in his lawyer's office in a Detroit suburb in 1992. The romance with pizza mogul Tom Monaghan had gone very, very sour and legal remedies were being sought.

Monaghan was hemorrhaging money from all his ventures and decided to sell the Tigers. At the time, there was some conjecture that he wouldn't be left with a pot to pizza in. Instead of telling his top executives, Bo and Jim Campbell, directly, however, he did it by long-distance telephone. As part of the terms of sale, they were out.

Campbell had been in Cooperstown where he was attending the Hall of Fame installation of Hal Newhouser. He was

Players and fans alike were thankful Bo stuck around after he retired as head coach so they could see for themselves the man who helped make Michigan, Michigan.

nearing retirement anyhow, but Bo was just 63 and still full of the old paprika. He was in his third year as president of the Tigers and had what he thought was a lifetime employment contract with Monaghan.

He was accustomed to dealing with Don Canham, who renewed his contract annually with a handshake. Money was never the issue, anyhow. Loyalty was. Now here he was in a lawyer's office, for God's sake, trying to get what he thought was his.

I never saw the man look so discomfited before or after. This wasn't his style or his turf at all. The terms of his settlement with Monaghan were never revealed, but I hope he got a good one just to make up for the embarrassment of this day.

Bo and Campbell had a great relationship. They were both Ohio boys, Bo from hardscrabble Barberton and Campbell from, as he put it, the "more genteel community" of Huron— which in some odd trick of geography was on Lake Erie.

Both had grown up as avid Cleveland Indians fans with Bob Feller as their all-time idol. Bo went on to become a fairly promising left-handed pitcher at Miami University, while Campbell played the outfield at Ohio State.

It was always Bo's contention that they had faced each other once and that in Campbell's only time at bat against him he struck him out. Campbell indignantly denied that any such thing had ever occurred. Or at least he didn't remember it.

Bo got in the last lick, though. He delivered one of the eulogies at Campbell's funeral in 1996 and insisted that his version of the story was right. "And no one can contradict me now," he said.

For a brief period after coaching, Bo became a TV network analyst, the second man in the booth during games. It didn't work out. He usually had to be prompted by the play-by-play guy to say something.

It was very strange because when it came to football he was the most garrulous of men, and his knowledge of the game's interior mechanics was encyclopedic.

I always felt he could never stop being a coach, even in the broadcast booth. He simply would get so involved in the game that he forgot to talk.

He understood, for example, that the defensive scheme Jim Herrmann had cooked up during the 1997 championship season could not long survive. In fact, he feared that Wisconsin coach Barry Alvarez, whom he deeply respected, might figure it out by the next to last game of the regular season. The Badgers did give Michigan one of its toughest games of the year, with the Wolverines holding on for dear life against their option attack.

"Y'see, when you commit your end and outside linebacker to the run, that leaves only an inside linebacker to cover the quarterback and the trailer with no backup," he said in a tutorial with me after that season. "A good option quarterback can hang that guy out to dry."

As soon as Michigan faced such a quarterback, in Syracuse's Donovan McNabb, he made mincemeat of the defense. But that was in 1998, when the championship trophy was safely in its case.

He never made excuses for anything. When Ernie Harwell was fired as the Tigers announcer—a move that was rescinded a few years later by popular demand—Bo took the blame for it. Almost instantly his popularity plummeted. One idol had collided with another and public support universally backed Ernie.

A few insiders knew that the bonehead move actually was engineered by Jim Long, the top executive at the Tigers' primary broadcast outlet, WJR radio. One of Bo's strengths was that he knew what he didn't know. So when Long started talking about demographics and new sponsorship deals, he deferred to his judgment.

While Long ducked out of the way for several days, Bo was savaged by commentators in every media, including this one. I still contend that as president of the Tigers, the ultimate responsibility rested with him. But Bo never tried to shift the blame and he took the blows, until Long finally decided to come out from under his bed and confess.

Bo lost a lot of friends during his tenure with the Tigers, especially with his abrupt and frequently ham-fisted campaign to replace Tiger Stadium. But he never backed off. He didn't know how.

But he was consistent in his beliefs. Three months before his death he returned to Barberton for the last time and spoke to the high school football team.

"It was really neat," said coach Jay Glaze. "He's a legend and even my kids, most of whom weren't even born when he quit coaching, understood that. His message was simple: Keep working hard because hard work pays off, and that football can be a vehicle to success."

As far as Bo was concerned, nothing would ever change that. He preached it every day of his life.

Bo coached at three schools in the Big Ten and two in the tough Mid-America Conference. But his first stop as an assistant was at tiny Presbyterian College, in South Carolina. It was only for a year but he always spoke of it with nostalgic fondness, even though it was remote from his other life experiences.

"I lived with one of the nicest families in town in a beautiful old mansion for 25 bucks a month plus breakfast," he said. "It was one of those places where they'd actually stop for tea in the afternoon.

"I had a choice of salary plans. Either a straight $3,600 a year or $3,400 with unlimited cafeteria rights. I went for the second option. It was great and they even let me eat with the basketball team."

Bo had a way of touching the heart and soul of just about every player he came into contact with at Michigan.

Despite the idyll in Dixie, Bo was rockbound Midwest, and for him the only goal worth achieving was the Rose Bowl. Although he was instrumental in getting the Big Ten to open up to other postseason games, he always viewed the Orange and Sugar and Fiesta bowls as consolation prizes, at best.

"When I was growing up in Ohio," he said, "the agreement with the Big Ten was in place and you'd look forward to New Year's Day to listen on the radio to Michigan or Ohio State or whoever was playing out there. When they started televising the games it was even better.

"You'd be sitting in the cold and snow and they'd be out there playing football in the sunshine. It was unbelievable. For me all the talk about national championships could never replace the sense of accomplishment of going to the Rose Bowl."

In the 1970s, Michigan and Ohio State totally dominated the Big Ten. Between 1968 and 1981, no other team went to Pasadena. Afterward, it was usually a dogfight as those two schools came back to the pack.

Most coaches understood that the NCAA-mandated cutback in football scholarships was mostly responsible. Players who once could be given such grants were now going to other schools. Instead of making do with the table scraps from the elite schools, by the late 1990s places like Boise State and Texas Christian were turning out powerhouses that could compete on an even level with most teams.

But Bo, typically, went beyond the obvious in explaining what had happened.

"It isn't only the games that are affected, it's the practices," he said. "You keep a team sharp with competitive practices. But when you're limited to the number of really good players, the quality of the practices falls off. That's why so many upsets occur."

For a coach to whom practice was akin to a religious rite, the connection was obvious.

Back in the '70s, alumni could be more actively involved in recruiting than they are now. The NCAA clamped down on the practice in the wake of many abuses, most of them involving under-the-table payoffs to promising kids.

Dr. Eugene Rontal, most noted in recent years for designing the protective face mask that enabled Richard Hamilton to continue playing for the Detroit Pistons during their 2004

As a final fitting legacy, Bo raised a good chunk of the $12 million to pay for Schembechler Hall, which was named in his honor.

championship run, was then a student assistant with the football team.

"I was fascinated by sports medicine at a time when it wasn't recognized as a specialty," he says. "So I got to know Bo a little and when I left to finish my medical training at the University of Minnesota, I told him that I'd look for some prospects. He said that would be fine, but from his tone I knew he was humoring me.

"But I took it seriously, and while I was in Minneapolis I heard about this kid playing in a little high school in the town of Crystal. I went to take a look, and he just dominated the game as a defensive tackle. He was kind of under the radar for most of the major schools, so I wrote to Bo about him. He actually did send one of the assistant coaches up to take a look.

"Well, they ended up recruiting Jeff Perlinger and he started for Michigan for three years. He was All–Big 10 in 1974. After that, he was always asking me to keep an eye out, and we became close friends. Once you proved that you knew your stuff with Bo, you were in."

The Schembechler era is usually recalled as a time when Michigan simply throttled most teams. Of the 194 games Bo won at Michigan, 163 were by seven points or more.

But his record in the other games was 31–33–5, which is why triumph was so often mingled with pain in memories of those years. No fewer than 12 of those games were lost with less than five minutes to play.

Everyone can recite the best wins: The 1969 Ohio State game. Anthony Carter's miraculous catch and run as time ran out against Indiana in 1979. The first Rose Bowl win against Washington in 1981.

But equally well remembered are the last-minute Rose Bowl loss to Stanford in 1972. The head-banging goal-line failure against Ohio State that same year. The field goals sailing just wide at Columbus in 1974 and at West Lafayette in 1976—the latter one dropping Michigan from number one after eight consecutive weeks. Miami coming back from 30–14 in the fourth quarter in 1988.

The other stat to remember, though, is that in Bo's tenure at Michigan it lost a grand total of 13 games by more than a touchdown—and four of those came during the injury-riddled 1984 season.

Like most of the greatest coaches, he seldom lost. He just ran out of time.

CHAPTER 13

The 21 Seasons of Bo

1969

Captain: Jim Mandich; QB: Don Moorhead

Date	Opponent	Ranking	Location	Score
9/20	Vanderbilt	—	H	42–14
9/27	Washington	20	H	45–7
10/4	Missouri	13	H	17–40
10/11	Purdue	—	H	31–20
10/18	MSU	13	A	12–23
10/25	Minnesota	—	A	35–9
11/1	Wisconsin	20	H	35–7
11/8	Illinois	18	A	57–0
11/15	Iowa	14	A	51–6
11/22	Ohio State	12	H	24–12
12/1	USC	7	(Rose Bowl)	3–10

Final Ranking: 9

Don Canham called it "the game that changed Michigan football." Bo said that "from that day forward everybody knew Michigan was back. And you better be ready to deal with us." On November 22, 1969, everything changed. After almost two decades of indifference, the Wolverines once again were part of the college football elite, and they have never looked back.

A lackluster 3–2 start gave little indication of what was ahead. Even after mauling their next four opponents by a combined score of 178–22, Michigan was still regarded as a minimal impediment to the machine Woody Hayes had assembled in Columbus.

Win or lose, Michigan already had clinched a Rose Bowl trip because of the no-repeat rule then in effect. But to Bo it was win or else, and he had convinced his players that they could.

Defensive back Barry Pierson in his finest hour intercepted three passes and returned a punt 60 yards to set up the touchdown that gave Michigan a first-half lead it would not surrender. In the scoreless second half, Michigan simply beat down OSU, forcing the Buckeyes into an uncomfortable and ineffective passing game that led to seven turnovers.

Even a Rose Bowl defeat following Schembechler's heart attack on the eve of the game could not dim the incredible achievement of his first season.

1970

Captains: Don Moorhead and Henry Hill; QB: Moorhead

Date	Opponent	Ranking	Location	Score
9/19	Arizona	8	H	20–9
9/26	Washington	10	A	17–3
10/3	Texas A&M	9	H	14–10
10/10	Purdue	7	A	29–0
10/17	MSU	6	H	34–20
10/24	Minnesota	5	H	39–13
10/31	Wisconsin	5	A	29–15
11/7	Illinois	5	H	42–0
11/14	Iowa	5	H	55–0
11/21	Ohio State	4	A	9–20

Final Ranking: 9

No longer a surprise team, Michigan was ranked in the top 10 all season. Contrary to the myth, however, their fans did not flock back all at once. Michigan State was the only home sellout and the final game with Iowa drew just 66,000 to the Big House. Texas A&M was the only real test on the schedule, with Michigan pulling it with just three minutes to play.

This time, however, Woody was waiting back in Columbus, and he was locked and loaded. OSU had another undefeated team with a roster that was still full of stars. The Buckeyes were ranked fifth, however, to Michigan's fourth.

"Going to the Rose Bowl was not the main thought on our minds," Hayes said afterward. "It was avenging last year's loss."

Which he did. It was the biggest margin Hayes ran up against Bo in their 10 head-to-head meetings.

1971

Captains: Frank Gusich and Guy Murdock; QB: Tom Slade

Date	Opponent	Ranking	Location	Score
9/11	Northwestern	4	A	21–6
9/18	Virginia	4	H	56–0
9/25	UCLA	4	H	38–0
10/2	Navy	2	H	46–0
10/9	MSU	2	A	24–13
10/16	Illinois	2	H	35–6
10/23	Minnesota	3	A	35–7
10/30	Indiana	3	H	61–7
11/6	Iowa	3	H	63–7
11/13	Purdue	3	A	20–17
11/20	Ohio State	3	H	10–7
1/1	Stanford	4	(Rose Bowl)	12–13

Final Ranking: 6

Some of the edge was off the rematch in Ann Arbor. While Michigan again was pounding every team on its schedule, Ohio State came into the game 6–3 and unranked.

After a three-year run of 20–1 in the Big Ten, Woody had lost his stars and was in a rebuilding mode. Nevertheless, Michigan almost made an uncharacteristic stumble. Only a last-minute Dana Coin field goal against Purdue the week before the OSU game preserved its undefeated season.

This was the game, however, that proved the cliché about records meaning nothing when rivals face each other. Hayes had his underdog squad pumped up, and with little more than two minutes to play they were clinging to a 7–3 lead. But Billy Taylor barreled in with the winning score on his last carry at the Big House. Michigan fans still treasure Bob Ufer's exuberant call of "Touchdown Billy Taylor! Touchdown Billy Taylor!"

A controversial Michigan interception on the game's last play sealed it, leading to the famous photograph of Hayes hurling the sideline yard markers at the officials in a rage.

The team's flaw, however, was that it had virtually no passing game. Bo understood the burden he was placing on his quarterback and always said he was especially impressed by the play of Tom Slade. He was even more impressed by the fact that after going 11–1 Slade ungrudgingly accepted a backup role to Dennis Franklin in the two seasons that followed. On the week of his death Bo had, in fact, attended Slade's funeral.

Once more, however, the powerful Michigan running game was checked in the Rose Bowl against an 8–3 Stanford team. With the score tied 10–10 in the fourth quarter, a Coin field-goal attempt fell short. When Stanford tried to run the ball out of its end zone, Ed Shuttlesworth made the tackle for a safety.

But quarterback Don Bunce brought the heavy underdogs down the field, and with just 16 seconds to play, a field goal ended Michigan's undefeated season, 13–12.

1972

Captains: Tom Coyle and Randy Logan; QB: Dennis Franklin

Date	Opponent	Ranking	Location	Score
9/16	Northwestern	11	H	7–0
9/23	UCLA	12	A	26–9
9/30	Tulane	8	H	41–7
10/7	Navy	5	H	35–7
10/14	MSU	5	H	10–0
10/21	Illinois	6	A	31–7
10/28	Minnesota	5	H	42–0
11/4	Indiana	4	A	21–7
11/11	Iowa	4	A	31–0
11/18	Purdue	3	H	9–6
11/25	Ohio State	3	A	11–14

Final Ranking: 6

It almost seemed like a repeat of last year. Once again, Michigan swept through its season prior to the finale, this time behind brilliant sophomore quarterback Dennis Franklin and the power running of Ed Shuttlesworth. And once again, Purdue almost undid them in the 10th week, with a Mike Lantry field goal pulling it out with one minute to play.

The best defensive unit ever assembled by Bo, anchored by tackle Dave Gallagher and defensive backs Randy Logan and Dave Brown, had given up just 43 points all season.

The difference was, however, that OSU was well stocked again at 8–1, with a number nine national ranking, and the game was back in Columbus.

Two goal-line stands by the Buckeyes defense decided it. In the second quarter, with Michigan trailing 7–3, Bo passed up the field goal and ran four straight plays to try to get the lead. The last attempt fell short by inches.

Then in the fourth quarter with Michigan trailing by three, Bo again refused to kick and go for the tie. Instead, Franklin was stopped at the 1-yard line. OSU had the win and the date with Southern California in the Rose Bowl.

To many it typified Schembechler's stubborn reliance on the run at all costs. But he was facing a coach who knew how to stop the run at all costs. "If you can't make one yard when the game is on the line, you don't deserve to win," was all he had to say about that.

1973

Captains: Dave Gallagher and Paul Seal; QB: Dennis Franklin

Date	Opponent	Ranking	Location	Score
9/15	Iowa	5	A	31–7
9/22	Stanford	5	H	47–10
9/29	Navy	4	H	14–0
10/6	Oregon	5	H	24–0
10/13	MSU	5	A	31–0
10/20	Wisconsin	4	H	35–6
10/27	Minnesota	4	A	34–7
11/3	Indiana	4	H	49–13
11/10	Illinois	4	H	21–6
11/17	Purdue	4	A	34–9
11/24	Ohio State	4	H	10–10

Final Ranking: 6

This turned out to be the most bitter of Bo's 21 seasons. The Big Ten voted to ignore its own no-repeat Rose Bowl rule, and in so doing changed the course of college football.

No team had come within two touchdowns of Michigan all season. Ohio State was also undefeated and the game was once more the marquee matchup of the regular schedule.

A record Michigan Stadium crowd watched OSU jump off to a 10–0 first-half lead. But the Wolverines pounded their way back into it, and just as in 1972, the game resolved itself with Michigan facing a fourth down inside the Buckeyes 10. Trailing 10–3 in the fourth quarter with 10 minutes still to play, Bo once again passed up the field goal and went for the touchdown and the tie. This time, however, Franklin made it all the way to the end zone on the run.

A 44-yard field-goal attempt in the last seconds by Mike Lantry was short. But the 10–10 tie should have given Michigan the bid to the Rose Bowl. Franklin's collarbone was broken in the fourth quarter, though, and Big Ten Commissioner Wayne Duke, shuddering at the possibility of yet another loss to the Pac 10, urged the conference athletics directors to back Ohio State.

Michigan went home with a 10–0–1 record and Schembechler's outrage knew no bounds. He forced a change in bowl eligibility rules in the Big Ten. Starting with the 1975 season, teams other than the conference champion could accept bowl bids other than the Rose.

1974

Captains: David Brown and Dennis Franklin; QB: Franklin

Date	Opponent	Ranking	Location	Score
9/14	Iowa	6	H	24–7
9/21	Colorado	6	H	31–0
9/28	Navy	5	H	52–0
10/5	Stanford	4	A	27–16
10/12	MSU	4	H	21–7
10/19	Wisconsin	3	A	24–20
10/26	Minnesota	3	H	49–0
11/2	Indiana	3	A	21–7
11/9	Illinois	4	A	14–6
11/16	Purdue	3	H	51–0
11/23	Ohio State	3	A	10–12

Final Ranking: 3

For the fifth straight year, Michigan went into the Ohio State game with a perfect record. Rob Lytle emerged as a big-time running back to complement Franklin's option wizardry, while six starters on defense made the All–Big 10 team. A few critics began to carp that Bo's run-intensive offense was "dull and boring," but it was annihilating everyone in the conference.

Except for Ohio State, which once more thwarted Michigan's Rose Bowl dreams and ended its 20-game unbeaten streak. Michigan held the Buckeyes without a touchdown, all their points coming on four field goals by Tom Klaban.

But another failed attempt by Lantry in the fourth quarter, this one from 23 yards, was ruled wide left—although Bo insisted it had passed high over the upright and that officials simply refused to make the call in Columbus. Franklin ended his career with a record of 30–2–1 and never went to a bowl game.

1975

Captains: Kirk Lewis and Don Dufek; QB: Rick Leach

Date	Opponent	Ranking	Location	Score
9/13	Wisconsin	2	A	23–6
9/20	Stanford	2	H	19–19
9/27	Baylor	9	H	14–14
10/4	Missouri	12	H	31–7
10/11	MSU	8	A	16–6
10/18	Northwestern	7	H	69–0
10/25	Indiana	7	H	55–7
11/1	Minnesota	7	A	28–21
11/8	Purdue	6	H	28–0
11/15	Illinois	4	A	21–15
11/22	Ohio State	4	H	14–21
1/1	Oklahoma	5	(Orange Bowl)	6–14

Final Ranking: 8

Any anticipated letdown after the graduation of Franklin didn't materialize. Instead, Rick Leach stepped right in, the first freshman to start at quarterback in Michigan history. He would remain there for four years.

A few early bumps, two nonconference ties, left Michigan out of the top 10 for the first time in three seasons. But as Leach gained traction and a young, tough offensive line—sparked by Mike Kenn and Walt Downing—rounded into form, Bo soon had the machine rolling once more.

The program passed another landmark. The Indiana game was the last one played at the Big House before a crowd of less than 100,000. For the first season ever, Michigan would play before one million people, at home and on the road. Canham's marketing and Bo's string of successes finally was filling all those seats.

The only thing missing was a closing win over Woody. For the fourth straight year, the season ended on a sour note. Pete Johnson scored his third touchdown of the game with two minutes left after an interception, and unbeaten Ohio State rolled on to Pasadena.

This time, though, there was some consolation. Michigan made its first trip to another bowl, playing top-ranked Oklahoma in the Orange. The Sooners took the national championship with a 14–6 win. A woozy Leach was on the sideline for most of the third quarter after taking a forearm to the head.

1976

Captains: Rob Lytle, Calvin O'Neal, and Kirk Lewis; QB: Rick Leach

Date	Opponent	Ranking	Location	Score
9/11	Wisconsin	2	H	40–27
9/18	Stanford	1	H	51–0
9/25	Navy	1	H	70–14
10/2	Wake Forest	1	H	31–0
10/9	MSU	1	H	42–10
10/16	Northwestern	1	A	38–7
10/23	Indiana	1	A	35–0
10/30	Minnesota	1	H	45–0
11/6	Purdue	1	A	14–16
11/13	Illinois	4	H	38–7
11/20	Ohio State	4	A	22–0
1/1	USC	2	(Rose Bowl)	6–14

Final Ranking: 3

Finally, a number one ranking for a Schembechler team. Michigan held the top spot for eight straight weeks. But a shocking upset at Purdue in week nine, with a potential game-winning field goal sailing wide in the last seconds, ended another championship dream.

This team was an offensive masterpiece. Michigan crushed its nonconference opponents by a combined score of 152–14 and averaged almost 39 points a game during the regular schedule. The real stunner was that wing back Jim Smith was named to several All-America teams, the first time a wide receiver had done that under the Schembechler regime.

Even an eighth-ranked Ohio State squad could not contain Michigan this time. Michigan ended the years of frustration and finally returned to the Rose Bowl by pounding the

Buckeyes 22–0 before their silenced home crowd. It was the first time Bo had won in Columbus and the first time in 12 years OSU was shut out. After a scoreless first half, OSU wilted under the pounding of Rob Lytle and Russell Davis.

Not so much Southern California. The third-ranked Trojans smothered Michigan's seemingly unstoppable offense, limiting it to a second-quarter touchdown by Lytle. It was now 0–3 for Bo in Pasadena.

1977

Captains: Dwight Hicks and Walt Downing; QB: Rick Leach

Date	Opponent	Ranking	Location	Score
9/10	Illinois	2	A	37–9
9/17	Duke	1	H	21–9
9/24	Navy	1	H	14–7
10/1	Texas A&M	3	H	41–3
10/8	MSU	3	A	24–14
10/15	Wisconsin	1	H	56–0
10/22	Minnesota	1	A	0–16
10/29	Iowa	6	H	23–6
11/5	Northwestern	6	H	63–20
11/12	Purdue	6	A	40–7
11/19	Ohio State	5	H	14–6
1/2	Washington	4	(Rose Bowl)	20–27

Final Ranking: 9

A retooled offense gave Leach more of an opportunity to pass. Michigan again took over the number one spot and held it off and on for four weeks. But once more one of its downtrodden conference competitors, in this case Minnesota, rose up to derail the express. Even more shocking, it was the first shutout of Michigan in Bo's tenure and the first time it had happened in 10 years.

His assistant coaches reported that Bo was so staggered by the defeat that he redoubled their workload, convinced that even Northwestern was capable of stopping his offense. Michigan won that game 63–20.

As usual, the OSU game decided the conference championship and for the second straight year Michigan held the Buckeyes without a touchdown. It was also the first time since 1950–51 that Michigan had beaten OSU in consecutive seasons.

But there was always the Rose Bowl to blight things. It was a new opponent, Washington, but that only seemed to make matters worse. The 13th-ranked Huskies rolled to a 24–0 lead before Leach began a furious second-half comeback. Michigan closed to within a touchdown before a pass that tantalizingly hung on Stan Edwards's shoulder pad was intercepted at the goal line in the final minute.

1978

Captains: Russell Davis and Jerry Meter; QB: Rick Leach

Date	Opponent	Ranking	Location	Score
9/16	Illinois	4	H	31–0
9/23	Notre Dame	5	A	28–14
9/30	Duke	4	H	52–0
10/7	Arizona	3	H	21–17
10/14	MSU	5	H	15–24
10/21	Wisconsin	9	A	42–0
10/28	Minnesota	8	H	42–10
11/4	Iowa	8	A	34–0
11/11	Northwestern	7	A	59–14
11/18	Purdue	7	H	24–6
11/25	Ohio State	6	A	14–3
1/1	USC	5	(Rose Bowl)	10–17

Final Ranking: 5

Same old script. A cakewalk through most of the schedule and disaster in Pasadena. This time the midseason upset was administered by Michigan State, the first loss to the Spartans since Bo's first year.

This was a deeply talented MSU team, with Kirk Gibson at wide receiver and Darryl Rogers as coach. Rogers would further endear himself to Michigan fans by referring to them as "arrogant asses." (He would later coach the Detroit Lions for a few disastrous seasons and famously exclaim: "What does a guy have to do to get fired around here?")

Another new wrinkle was the addition of Notre Dame to the schedule for the first time since 1943. Leach recovered from a sore ankle to lead a second-half surge that defeated the Irish in a matchup that would immediately become an annual classic.

MSU was ineligible for a bowl, so even though Michigan ended up in a tie with them for the title it was the Wolverines who headed back to Pasadena for the third straight year. They muffled Ohio State and Woody Hayes along the way, also stopping them without a touchdown for the third straight year. Leach threw two touchdown passes in the game, as if to punctuate Bo's newfound willingness to fling the football.

This was the last game between the two legendary coaches, ending their confrontations with Bo holding a 5–4–1 edge. Hayes was fired during the off-season after his contretemps with a Clemson player in the Gator Bowl.

For Michigan, it was more anguish in the Rose. This was the year of the phantom touchdown, with USC running back Charles White given credit for scoring when the ball clearly had left his grasp on the 2-yard line. Bo's howls of protest did no good and his postseason record went to 0–6.

1979

Captains: John Arbeznik and Ron Simpkins; QB: B.J. Dickey

Date	Opponent	Ranking	Location	Score
9/8	Northwestern	7	H	49–7
9/15	Notre Dame	6	H	10–12
9/22	Kansas	11	H	28–7
9/29	California	11	A	14–10
10/6	MSU	11	A	21–7
10/13	Minnesota	11	H	31–21
10/20	Illinois	11	A	27–7
10/27	Indiana	10	H	27–21
11/3	Wisconsin	10	H	54–0
11/10	Purdue	10	A	21–24
11/17	Ohio State	13	H	15–18
12/28	North Carolina	14	(Gator Bowl)	15–17

Final Ranking: 18

As they must for all men, things caught up with Bo in 1979. Leach was gone and his understudy, B.J. Dickey, was not nearly as accomplished. An early loss to Notre Dame bounced Michigan out of the top 10 and they never got higher than 10th the rest of the way.

One result of this, however, was that Bo forsook the option and countenanced a pure drop-back passer. John Wangler became his starter in the season's second half. A big reason for that was freshman Anthony Carter, who quickly emerged as a dangerous big-play receiver. Wangler's desperation TD heave to Carter as time ran out in the Indiana game was among the most dramatic finishes in Michigan history—at least, on the positive side. Or as announcer Bob Ufer put it, "Anthony Carter ran like a penguin with a hot herring in his cummerbund."

But pesky Purdue knocked off the Wolverines in week 10 and undefeated Ohio State, now coached by Earle Bruce, finished

Anthony Carter first electrified crowds at the Big House during his freshman season in 1979.

the job. The Buckeyes were also reborn as a passing team, with Art Schlichter throwing the ball around in a manner that would have curled Woody's hair. It was a blocked punt, however, that led to the winning score, just the sort of error that Schembechler teams were not supposed to make.

The two late losses placed Michigan third in the conference, the first time Bo failed to finish either first or second in the Big Ten. The 8–3 record was good only for a bid to the Gator Bowl.

While some members of the media moaned about the proud Wolverines going to a "fleabag bowl," even there Bo could not prevail. Carter caught two long touchdown passes, one from Wangler and one from Dickey, but a two-point conversion try to tie the game in the fourth quarter went awry and another bowl was down the drain.

1980

Captains: Andy Cannavino and George Lilja; QB: John Wangler

Date	Opponent	Ranking	Location	Score
9/13	Northwestern	11	H	17–10
9/20	Notre Dame	14	A	27–29
9/27	South Carolina	17	H	14–17
10/4	California	—	H	38–13
10/11	MSU	—	H	27–23
10/18	Minnesota	—	A	37–14
10/25	Illinois	—	H	45–14
11/1	Indiana	18	A	35–0
11/8	Wisconsin	12	A	24–0
11/15	Purdue	11	H	26–0
11/22	Ohio State	10	A	9–3
1/1	Washington	5	(Rose Bowl)	23–6

Final Ranking: 4

The previous season's malaise seemed to be lingering on. A struggling win over feeble Northwestern was followed by fourth-quarter losses to Notre Dame and (gasp!) South Carolina—the kind of school that was usually scheduled as Big House cannon fodder.

Bo hit the roof when he heard murmurs that football "wasn't fun" anymore for his team and he decided to coach "attitude" the rest of the year. The brisk, head-banging approach worked. Michigan didn't lose again. After four weeks of being completely out of the rankings it began to ascend as November arrived. Not a single touchdown was scored against them in the final five games.

The entire offensive line of Ed Muransky, Bubba Paris, Kurt Becker, and George Lilja was named All–Big Ten, while Anthony Carter made several All-America teams as a sophomore. He caught the touchdown pass from Wangler that broke a tie and defeated Ohio State, taking Michigan back to Pasadena for the fourth time in five years. It was also the fourth time during that span in which OSU could not cross the Michigan goal line.

And in Pasadena, the New Year finally began in sunshine. Washington held Carter without a catch in the first half. But with explicit instructions from Bo to get the ball to him, Wangler passed Michigan to its first Rose Bowl win in 16 years. "We're not leaving with our tails between our legs this time," said the coach. It was the first time at Michigan his season had ended with a win.

1981

Captains: Kurt Becker and Robert Thompson; QB: Steve Smith

Date	Opponent	Ranking	Location	Score
9/12	Wisconsin	1	A	14–21
9/19	Notre Dame	11	H	25–7
9/26	Navy	7	H	21–16
10/3	Indiana	8	A	38–17
10/10	MSU	6	A	38–20
10/17	Iowa	6	H	7–9
10/24	Northwestern	18	H	38–0
10/31	Minnesota	15	A	34–13
11/7	Illinois	12	H	70–21
11/14	Purdue	11	A	28–10
11/21	Ohio State	7	H	9–14
12/31	UCLA	16	(Bluebonnet Bowl)	33–14

Final Ranking: 12

This was one of the most disappointing seasons in Bo's career. A team that was ranked first in the nation was knocked off by Wisconsin in the season opener at Madison.

Veteran players could not recall practices more grueling than the ones that preceded Notre Dame on week two. But a solid smashing of the Irish seemed to indicate that things had been righted. This remained a star-studded team on offense, with Carter back for his junior year and Butch Woolfolk at tailback. But something just wasn't clicking.

A loss to Iowa at home was galling, and even a 70-point eruption against Bo's favorite whipping boys, Mike White's Illinois team, couldn't hide the deficiencies. With the Rose Bowl on the line again, Michigan was held to three field goals by OSU. It wasn't a vintage Ohio State matchup, either. In fact, for the first time since the 1967 season, it was another school, Iowa, that would be going to Pasadena.

Michigan ended up playing UCLA in the Houston Bluebonnet Bowl, a trip marked primarily by job offers to Bo from Texas A&M boosters. He turned them down, but he also irritated UCLA coach Terry Donohue, who felt he played his regulars a bit longer than necessary in a game that had been decided. That attitude would figure prominently during the next season.

1982

Captains: Anthony Carter, Paul Girgash, and Robert Thompson; QB: Steve Smith

Date	Opponent	Ranking	Location	Score
9/11	Wisconsin	12	H	20–9
9/18	Notre Dame	10	A	17–23
9/25	UCLA	20	H	27–31
10/2	Indiana	—	H	24–10
10/9	MSU	—	H	31–17
10/16	Iowa	—	A	29–7
10/23	Northwestern	—	A	49–14
10/30	Minnesota	20	H	52–14
11/6	Illinois	15	A	16–10
11/13	Purdue	14	H	52–21
11/20	Ohio State	13	A	14–24
1/1	UCLA	19	(Rose Bowl)	14–24

Final Ranking: unranked

For the first time since Bo's arrival, a Michigan team finished the season unranked. Moreover, Terry Donohue's UCLA team became the first, and only, team to beat Bo twice in the same season.

A perplexing state of affairs, although Michigan once again headed to the Rose Bowl even with a loss in Columbus. Ohio State was far from par. For the first time since 1967, neither team was even ranked in the top 10 when they met and Michigan already had the Pasadena trip wrapped up.

The Wolverines also played as if the game were an afterthought, turning the ball over six times. The last one came on a fumble deep in their own territory in the fourth quarter, and a Tim Spencer run put the Buckeyes ahead to stay.

The Rose Bowl only brought more of the same. UCLA was unranked going into the game but took an early lead. When quarterback Steve Smith had to leave with a shoulder separation, the Michigan situation turned dire. His inexperienced replacement, Dave Hall, had thrown just 14 passes all year. When one of his tosses was intercepted in the fourth quarter, the Bruins took it in to wrap up the game.

1983

Captains: Stefan Humphries and John Lott; QB: Steve Smith

Date	Opponent	Ranking	Location	Score
9/10	Washington State	6	H	20–17
9/17	Washington	8	A	24–25
9/24	Wisconsin	17	A	38–21
10/1	Indiana	14	H	43–18
10/8	MSU	14	A	42–0
10/15	Northwestern	13	H	35–0
10/22	Iowa	10	H	16–13
10/29	Illinois	8	A	6–16
11/5	Purdue	13	H	42–10
11/12	Minnesota	9	A	58–10
11/19	Ohio State	8	H	24–21
1/2	Auburn	8	(Sugar Bowl)	7–9

Final Ranking: 8

This was not one of Bo's most talented squads, although Stefan Humphries and center Tom Dixon were standouts on the offensive line. But a scrappy defense managed to keep the team in most games.

A narrow loss to Washington on the road was followed by a string of conference blowouts. But Illinois had finally come up with a balanced team that could stand up to the Wolverines. The Illini took them down at Champaign in a contest that decided the conference title.

Steve Smith, finishing his third season as starting quarterback, played one of his best games to get the win against Ohio State. He threw for two TDs, including a 67-yarder to Triando Markray, and then sneaked in himself to bring the team back from a 14–10 deficit.

The victory took Michigan to New Orleans. It was their first trip to the Sugar Bowl and matched them against All-American Bo Jackson's third-ranked Auburn squad. In this Battle of the Bos, the Wolverines held Auburn to three field goals, and Jackson later stated he had never been hit harder in his life. But with a late score Auburn dealt Michigan yet another bowl loss.

1984

Captains: Doug James and Mike Mallory; QB: Jim Harbaugh

Date	Opponent	Ranking	Location	Score
9/8	Miami (Florida)	14	H	22–14
9/15	Washington	3	H	11–20
9/22	Wisconsin	16	H	20–14
9/29	Indiana	14	A	14–6
10/6	MSU	13	H	7–19
10/13	Northwestern	—	H	31–0
10/20	Iowa	—	A	0–26
10/27	Illinois	—	H	26–18
11/3	Purdue	—	A	29–31
11/10	Minnesota	—	H	31–7
11/17	Ohio State	—	A	6–21
12/21	Brigham Young		(Holiday Bowl)	17–24

Final Ranking: unranked

Almost a total catastrophe. No season started off better, with a walloping of the previous year's national champions, Miami. No season ended worse, with a 6–6 record and an offense that could score just 14 more points than the defense allowed. Not a single member of the offensive unit made the All-Conference Team and Michigan plunged all the way to sixth place in the Big Ten, their worst finish ever under Bo.

Things became unraveled in week five when sophomore quarterback Jim Harbaugh was injured and had to sit out the rest of the season. This meant two other inexperienced players, Chris Zurbrugg and Russ Rein, had to be rushed in to run the team. Neither one ever started another game after this season.

While Michigan did manage to hold serve at home, they didn't win another road game the rest of the year. Iowa took them down 26–0, the most thorough drubbing Schembechler endured at Michigan. Then Ohio State, behind three touchdowns from Keith Byars, pounded them in Columbus to get the Rose Bowl bid.

Michigan did get a California trip, but it was to the San Diego Holiday Bowl to face undefeated Brigham Young. In this topsy-turvy year, the pass-happy Western Athletic Conference champion was the top-ranked team in the country. Even with a 6–5 record, however, Michigan was given the chance to topple the leaders.

They almost did the job, but couldn't protect a 17–10 lead in the fourth quarter. Robbie Bosco passed for more than 300 yards for the Cougars, including the winner with one minute and 23 seconds to play. Brigham Young was voted national champions almost by default, infuriating several major college coaches who felt their weak schedule and narrow victory over a weak Michigan team did not render them worthy.

1985

Captains: Brad Cochran, Eric Kattus, and Mike Mallory; QB: Jim Harbaugh

Date	Opponent	Ranking	Location	Score
9/14	Notre Dame	—	H	20–12
9/21	South Carolina	19	A	34–3
9/28	Maryland	12	H	20–0
10/5	Wisconsin	5	H	33–6
10/12	MSU	3	A	31–0
10/19	Iowa	2	A	10–12
10/26	Indiana	4	H	42–15
11/2	Illinois	4	A	3–3
11/9	Purdue	9	H	47–0
11/16	Minnesota	8	A	48–7
11/23	Ohio State	6	H	27–17
1/1	Nebraska	5	(Fiesta Bowl)	27–23

Final Ranking: 2

This was the first time Michigan entered the season unranked since 1969. That made it a season that ran exactly in reverse of the previous one, because the final number two ranking was the highest Bo ever achieved.

There had been whispers during the off-season. Michigan still won a lot more than it lost, but it was no longer sharing dominance in the Big Ten with Ohio State. It seemed to have come back to the pack. And 6–6? What was that? That made two years out of the last three Michigan finished the season unranked. Could it be that the game was passing Bo by?

But the disastrous 1984 campaign was soon shown to be an anomaly. With a healthy Harbaugh running the attack and Jamie Morris at tailback, this was once again a formidable offense. But the team's signature was its defense. With Mike Hammerstein, one of the best pass rushers ever to play at

Michigan, and a defensive backfield that started every game as a unit, Bo had his best defense in years, holding opponents to a combined total of 98 points.

A loss to top-ranked Iowa on the road on a field goal with two seconds to play, however, decided the Big Ten race. It was the first time Michigan was involved in a game that matched the number one and number two teams in the polls since 1943. It lost that one, too, to number one Notre Dame.

Harbaugh shattered most of Michigan's passing records in this season and threw three TD tosses against Ohio State, including a 77-yarder to John Kolesar that broke the game open. When asked if beating OSU was as satisfying as winning a bowl game, Bo replied: "Absolutely. Have you checked my record in the bowls?"

That record improved to 3–10 with a win over eighth-ranked Nebraska in the Fiesta Bowl. Trailing 14–3 at the half, Michigan's defense came out and forced the Cornhuskers into two fumbles and a blocked punt. The Wolverines scored 24 points in the third quarter and put the game away.

1986

Captains: Jim Harbaugh and Andy Moeller; QB: Harbaugh

Date	Opponent	Ranking	Location	Score
9/13	Notre Dame	3	A	24–23
9/20	Oregon State	3	H	31–12
9/27	Florida State	5	H	20–18
10/4	Wisconsin	4	A	34–17
10/11	MSU	4	H	27–6
10/18	Iowa	4	H	20–17
10/25	Indiana	4	A	38–14
11/1	Illinois	3	H	69–13
11/8	Purdue	3	A	31–7
11/15	Minnesota	2	H	17–20
11/22	Ohio State	6	A	26–24
12/6	Hawaii	4	A	27–10
1/1	Arizona State	4	(Rose Bowl)	15–22

Final Ranking: 8

Another Rose Bowl campaign, this one marked by no fewer than five games decided by three points or less. The Wolverines got back at Iowa by kicking the winning field goal as time ran out. But the sword cut back in week 10, that treacherous time just before the OSU game, when Minnesota upset them by the same 20–17 score in the same time frame.

Harbaugh and tailback Jamie Morris again were forces, working behind an offensive line that included Jumbo Elliott and John Vitale. The season featured the first meeting against Bobby Bowden's Florida State team and the first trip to Hawaii. That was a voyage Bo didn't care for at all since it took his jet-lagged team until the fourth quarter to take the lead against ordinary competition.

He also didn't care for the scheduling because for just the second time since 1935 Ohio State didn't conclude the regular season. (The other time was in 1942 because of the exigencies of wartime travel.) Still, the OSU game was a classic. Harbaugh had guaranteed a win after the previous week's upset by Minnesota, a move calculated to infuriate the Buckeyes and their 90,000 fans in the Horseshoe.

He kept his word. Morris rushed for 210 yards, but only a near miss on a last-second field goal iced the win for Michigan. "I'd have worried about it more if he didn't think we'd win," said Bo about his quarterback.

But the same old problems surfaced in the Rose Bowl. Michigan's running game was utterly stifled and the Sun Devils blanked them in the second half to send Bo to yet another Pasadena fizzle.

1987

Captains: Jamie Morris and Doug Mallory; QB: Demetrius Brown

Date	Opponent	Ranking	Location	Score
9/12	Notre Dame	9	H	7–26
9/19	Washington State	19	H	44–18
9/26	Long Beach State	14	H	49–0
10/3	Wisconsin	12	H	49–0
10/10	MSU	12	A	11–17
10/17	Iowa	—	H	37–10
10/24	Indiana	20	A	10–14
10/31	Northwestern	—	H	29–6
11/7	Minnesota	—	A	30–20
11/14	Illinois	—	A	17–14
11/21	Ohio State	—	H	0–23
1/2	Alabama	—	(Hall of Fame Bowl)	28–24

Final Ranking: 19

Time for a comedown as Bo had to replace another long-termer at quarterback. It was especially galling because the season featured the first loss to Indiana in 20 years as well as a loss to George Perles's Rose Bowl–bound Michigan State team. It was the first time the Spartans had gone to Pasadena since Bo entered the conference, and MSU's vote in the aftermath of the 1973 tie with Ohio State still irked him.

Earle Bruce was fired a few days before the Michigan game, a move unpopular with both players and athletics director Rich Bay, who resigned in protest. The Buckeyes were in the midst of a lackluster 6–4–1 season, but they came out and did the job against Michigan. Fittingly, the place-kicker who had missed the previous season's critical field goal, Matt Franz, sent it through this time for the win.

"There is no sweeter feeling than beating Michigan," said the sacked Bruce, still loyal to the scarlet and gray.

The fourth-place conference finish sent the Wolverines to Tampa, the Hall of Fame Bowl, and their first-ever meeting with another storied program, Alabama. But Bo had to stay at home. He underwent quadruple bypass surgery a few weeks before this game. It was one of the factors in his impending decision to call it a career.

Gary Moeller, his eventual successor, was acting head coach. Passing up a try for a tying field goal on a fourth-and-three at the Alabama 20, he had Brown loft a pass to John Kolesar in the farthest corner of the end zone for the win. Jamie Morris broke all school rushing records with a 234-yard day and a 4,393-yard career total.

1988

Captains: Mark Messner and John Vitale; QB: Michael Taylor

Date	Opponent	Ranking	Location	Score
9/10	Notre Dame	9	A	17–19
9/17	Miami (Florida)	15	H	30–31
9/24	Wake Forest	19	H	19–9
10/1	Wisconsin	19	A	62–14
10/8	MSU	17	H	17–3
10/15	Iowa	15	A	17–17
10/22	Indiana	20	H	31–6
10/29	Northwestern	15	A	52–7
11/5	Minnesota	14	H	22–7
11/12	Illinois	13	H	38–9
11/19	Ohio State	12	A	34–31
1/2	USC	11	(Rose Bowl)	22–14

Final Ranking: 4

An inauspicious start led unexpectedly to one of Bo's most satisfying years. Another tight loss to Notre Dame on a last-minute
field goal was followed by an even more galling loss to Miami in
the last 43 seconds.

Michigan had controlled the top-ranked Hurricanes for most
of the game, building a 30–14 lead in the fourth quarter. Then
Miami's passing game started to click, and with less than two
minutes to play it was down to 30–24. On a third-down pass that
would have retained possession for Michigan and iced the game,
Miami coach Jimmy Johnson talked officials into ruling that the
Wolverines receiver was juggling the ball when he stepped out of
bounds. Miami took the punt and drove right in for the score,
while Bo railed at the officials for a questionable call and sputtered at Johnson for pulling such gamesmanship on Michigan's
home field. That was supposed to be Bo's forte.

But that was one of the few lapses of the season. John Vitale
and Mike Husar led an offensive line that cleared the way for

Tony Boles and Leroy Hoard, while John Kolesar and Greg McMurtry were formidable wide receivers. Only a tie at Iowa marred the rest of the way.

Kolesar took the Ohio State game on his own shoulders and into his hands. With 92 seconds left after OSU had taken the lead, he returned the kickoff 59 yards. On the next play from scrimmage, he caught a touchdown pass from Demetrius Brown. Kolesar's historic heroics blunted a great comeback by the Buckeyes, who were down 20–0 at the half, for first-year coach John Cooper.

For a change, the best was yet to come. Bo finally got to walk out of the Rose Bowl and light a victory cigar as a winner against USC. Brown loosened up the defense just enough for the big Michigan ground attack to finally work in this bowl game. Hoard rushed for 142 yards and scored two fourth-quarter TDs, while the Trojans were shut out in the second half.

1989
Captains: J.J. Grant and Derrick Walker; QB: Michael Taylor

Date	Opponent	Ranking	Location	Score
9/16	Notre Dame	2	H	19–24
9/23	UCLA	5	A	24–23
9/30	Maryland	6	H	41–21
10/7	Wisconsin	5	H	24–0
10/14	MSU	5	A	10–7
10/21	Iowa	5	A	26–12
10/28	Indiana	5	H	38–10
11/4	Purdue	4	H	42–27
11/11	Illinois	3	A	24–10
11/18	Minnesota	3	A	49–15
11/25	Ohio State	3	H	28–18
1/1	USC	3	(Rose Bowl)	10–17

Final Ranking: 7

The final curtain, although no one, not even Bo, knew that until late in the year. Another shaky start was narrowly averted when a last-second field goal at the Rose Bowl beat UCLA in week two. That followed another crushing defeat by Notre Dame in the opener—the third instance when a number two Michigan team went up against the top-ranked team and faltered.

But there were no other slip-ups. The Wolverines roared undefeated through the Big Ten, just like old times, and ended up with a royal smashing of Ohio State. It was the first time any team had won two straight Big Ten titles outright since Michigan State accomplished it in 1965–66.

Top runner Tony Boles went down with a career-ending injury in midseason. But Jarrod Bunch, who scored twice against the Buckeyes, said that the running backs had dedicated that game to Boles. They scored all four Michigan TDs...again, just like old times.

There was also a peek at the future this season, as quarterback-in-waiting Elvis Grbac, the best pure passer at Michigan since Harbaugh, started four games.

Bo announced his retirement to a room filled with teary-eyed players two weeks before the Rose Bowl. But the storybook ending was not to be. A holding call on a fake punt, followed by an unsportsmanlike conduct penalty on Bo, forced Michigan to turn the ball over to USC. The Trojans came in for the winning touchdown with 70 seconds to play.

The unfortunate image of Bo screaming at the officials over the call, which he always insisted was bogus, and tripping on the phone wires along the sideline, was the last one the national TV audience had of him.

Notes

Chapter 2

"Don't you realize that hook on the wall..." Schembechler, Glenn and Ewald, Dan. *Michigan Memories: Inside Bo Schembechler's Football Scrapbook* (Chelsea: Clock Tower Press, 1998), p. 113.

"We must have started with about 150 guys..." Detroit News Staff. *A Legacy of Champions: The Story of the Men Who Built University of Michigan Football* (Farmington Hills: CTC Production and Sports, 1996), p. 122.

"When you'd go to his office first thing in the morning..." Ann Arbor News Staff. *Unrivaled: Michigan v. Ohio State* (Ann Arbor: Ann Arbor News, 2005), p. 45.

Chapter 3

"Bo posted the score of that 1968 game..." Emanuel, Greg. *The 100-Yard War: Inside the 100-Year-Old Michigan-Ohio Rivalry* (Hoboken: John Wiley & Sons, Inc, 2004), p. 96.

"After we went for a two-point conversion...." Ann Arbor News Staff. *Unrivaled: Michigan v. Ohio State* (Ann Arbor: Ann Arbor News, 2005), p. 49.

"Ohio State came into that game...." "In Memory: Pierson Runs 60 Yards Forever" *Detroit Free Press,* August 29, 1997, section D, p. 1.

"If Woody had a downfall...." Snook, Jeff, *What It Means To Be a Buckeye.* (Chicago: Triumph Books, 2003), p. 116.

"I swear it was like Bo was in our huddle..." Ann Arbor News Staff. *Unrivaled: Michigan v. Ohio State* (Ann Arbor: Ann Arbor News, 2005), p. 56.

"We started moving right through them..." Ann Arbor News Staff. *Unrivaled: Michigan v. Ohio State* (Ann Arbor: Ann Arbor News, 2005), p. 55.

"I have never looked at that film" Ann Arbor News Staff. *Unrivaled: Michigan v. Ohio State* (Ann Arbor: Ann Arbor News, 2005), p. 56.

Chapter 4

"I'd heard two things when I was being recruited..." "Archie Griffin Remembers Bo Schembechler," Ohio State Alumni Association Newsletter, November 2006.

"I was coaching at a Cleveland area high school..." "Detroit Lions React to Death of Michigan Hall of Fame Coach" (Detroit Lions, accessed November 2006); www.detroitlions.com.

"I played my first game at Michigan seven years after Bo..." "Detroit Lions React to Death of Michigan Hall of Fame Coach" (Detroit Lions, accessed November 2006); www.detroitlions.com.

Chapter 5

"We went into the 1980 season...." "Bo: Happy a Bond Still Exists with His Former Players," *The Detroit News*, January 12, 1989, section D, p. 5.

"We knew that sometime during the week..." Schembechler, Glenn and Ewald, Dan. *Michigan Memories: Inside Bo Schembechler's Football Scrapbook* (Chelsea, Michigan: Clock Tower Press, 1998), p. 15.

Chapter 6

"Bo demanded loyalty but..." Detroit News Staff. *A Legacy of Champions: The Story of the Men Who Built University of Michigan Football* (Farmington Hills, Michigan: CTC Production and Sports, 1996), ix.

"I was driving along Interstate 94..." Schembechler, Glenn and
Ewald, Dan. *Michigan Memories: Inside Bo Schembechler's Football
Scrapbook* (Chelsea: Clock Tower Press, 1998), Michigan
Memories p. 42.

"The following year Dennis Franklin was ready to play..." Falls,
Joe, *Man in Motion* (Ann Arbor: School-Tech Press, 1973) p.
112.

Chapter 7

"I interviewed Bo in 1996 for Blitz Magazine...." Paul, Alan,
"R.I.P. Bo Schembechler" (*SLAM Magazine,* accessed
November 20, 1996); Slamonline.com.

"The first thing I knew about it...." Wojciechowski, Gene,
"When Bo Called, Fisher and Majerus Listened" (accessed
November 18, 2006); www.ESPN.com

"Bo's approach definitely had an impact..." Wetzel, Dan,
"Remembering Schembechler" (Yahoo, accessed November
20, 2006); www.yahoosports.com

"I called them in to discuss the agent thing...." Detroit News
Staff. *A Legacy of Champions: The Story of the Men Who Built
University of Michigan Football* (Farmington Hills: CTC
Production and Sports, 1996), p. 151.

Chapter 8

"He was aware of everything that went on...." Ann Arbor News
Staff. *Unrivaled: Michigan v. Ohio State* (Ann Arbor: Ann Arbor
News, 2005), p. 111.

"There was a Labor Day ritual...." "Bo Leaves Memories Behind,"
Michigan Daily, December 21, 1989, section A, p. 1.

Chapter 9

"I escaped from Columbus....." "Remembering Bo," (*The
Columbus Dispatch,* accessed November 18);
www.dispatch.com.

"If Bo is not a winner...." Looney, Douglas S. "Schembechler's
the Name; Football's His Game," *Sports Illustrated,* September
14, 1981.

"Bo is oblivious to life..." Looney, Douglas S. "Schembechler's the Name; Football's His Game," *Sports Illustrated,* September 14, 1981.

"I was a captain of the Ohio State football team..." Ann Arbor News Staff. *Unrivaled: Michigan v. Ohio State* (Ann Arbor: Ann Arbor News, 2005), p. 111.

"Woody was famous for his hatred of Michigan...." (Bucknuts, accessed November 2005); www.bucknuts.com

"Woody was famous for his motivational speeches..." (Bucknuts, accessed November 2005); www.bucknuts.com

"Several times Bo would be sick..." *The Columbus Dispatch,* accessed November 19, 2006); www.dispatch.com.

"He met Elvis once..." "Memories of a Michigan Legend," *Detroit Free Press,* November 19, 2006, section A, p. 1.

Chapter 10

"The time it really washed over me..." "Bo: Happy a Bond Still Exists with His Former Players," *Detroit News,* January 12, 1989, section D, p. 5.

"I know how he felt and we even discussed it..." Fricke, Mark, "The Tom Osborne Interview," (Husker Press Box, accessed September 28, 1998); www.huskernews.com.

Chapter 11

"I sometimes suggested, perhaps...." Schembechler, Glenn and Ewald, Dan. *Michigan Memories: Inside Bo Schembechler's Football Scrapbook* (Chelsea: Clock Tower Press, 1998), p. 36.

"I cleaned out his locker...." Schembechler, Glenn and Ewald, Dan. *Michigan Memories: Inside Bo Schembechler's Football Scrapbook* (Chelsea: Clock Tower Press, 1998), p. 43.

"I was supposed to introduce Fleming...." Falls, Joe, *Man in Motion* (Ann Arbor: School-Tech Press, 1973), p. 18.